Friendship

from stress and stave off illness as well as facilitate convalescence. Weaving friendship connections should develop a stronger social fiber strengthening a sane, robust society in which individuals can flourish.

This volume considers what friendship is by exploring various types of relations and the social context in which they are embedded. The component parts of friendship are investigated with particular attention to the element of reciprocity. Reciprocal interaction is a pivotal concept in understanding relations. There is considerable superficial reference to the concept of reciprocity in numerous works on relations. Here the concept is explored more fully and developed and a schema of reciprocity is developed.

The part reciprocity plays in friendship is elaborated and friendship is viewed from both a real and an ideal standpoint.

Preface

Friendship is a relationship severely underrated in American society. Though a universal concept, the image and perceived value vary considerably across cultures and even within subsets of cultures.

The term friend has been used somewhat indiscriminately though core concepts of friendship in American culture imply a voluntary relationship. In our individualistic, advancement-oriented society, political and business relations are a close second to marriage in importance or even sometimes overshadow marriage. All other relations are subjugated.

Friendship is potentially a valuable relation. In American society friendship suffers from an absence of supportive sanction. Marriage is the premier relation and so accustomed are we to this prevailing sentiment that we ignore discussion about other significant relationships. Yet the Greeks, for example, and a number of cultures studied by anthropologists cited in this work, place friendship at the pinnacle of relationships. There is no intention here to question the salience of marriage in any schema of relationships. In fact friendship should support rather than supplant marriage.

What seems intriguing about friendship is its inclusive nature, whereas other relations often maintain exclusionary boundaries. It is possible for two people to be friends and have no other relational connections yet it is also possible to be siblings and friends, spouses and friends, colleagues and friends. Friendship is, in fact, more a relationship of *what* rather than *who* or *where*.

Years of studying friendship leave me questioning the social context inhibitors. A rich, robust relationship like friendship should have social sanctions, be celebrated, taught, through modeling and the like. Such is not the case. Although there is rarely public admission of lack of friends, there is also little visible dedication to developing and maintaining friends. Absence from work or family to be with friends is typically not viable. Yet unless children experience friendships and see they have value to adults, they are unlikely to continue friendships into adulthood. Adult behavior is also reflective of environment.

Friendship can be an elixir in this troubling world. One's present and future health, both physical and psychological, can be measured by and attributed to strong relational ties. Those who have friends are seen as healthy as compared to the friendless. Social and personal development are enhanced by friendship. Evidence is mounting that strong relational ties, i.e. friendship, may buffer people

Table of Contents

To my mother and father who were wonderful parents to me as a child and are wonderful friends for me as an adult.

Library of Congress Cataloging-in-Publication Data

Reohr, Janet Ruth, 1948–
    Friendship : an exploration of structure and process / Janet R.
Reohr.
      p. cm. — (Garland reference library of social science ; v.
431)
    Includes bibliographical references.
    ISBN 0–8240–7242–1 (alk. paper)
    1. Friendship. I. Title. II. Series.
BF575.F66R46   1991
302.3'4—dc20
                                       91–19930
                                          CIP

Printed on acid-free, 250-year-life paper
Manufactured in the United States of America

FRIENDSHIP
An Exploration of Structure and Process

Janet R. Reohr

GARLAND PUBLISHING, INC. • NEW YORK & LONDON
1991

FRIENDSHIP

GARLAND REFERENCE LIBRARY
OF SOCIAL SCIENCE
(VOL. 431)

Chapter 1

Friendship in Society

In American society today friendship is seen an an inconsequential relationship. Whereas in some cultures friendship is sanctioned, given a position of great value and publicly proclaimed through rites and ceremonies, in American society friendship is not similarly supported.

Friendship is a culturally patterned interpersonal relationship (DuBois, p. 3, 1955). The concept of friendship appears in all cultures but the expectations and behaviors of the relationship vary considerably. As with other types of relating, friendships are dependent upon the social context in which they are immersed. There are several main reasons for a distinctive American type of relating. The social, cultural, economic, and structural conditions present in this country influence the way people organize and perceive their lives. In addition, values held by Americans, and subsequent behaviors, influence relations. Values and behaviors today are dependent on present circumstances in this country and are also dependent on those values and beliefs held historically. Although there is a great divergence of cultural heritage, there are commonalties in American friendship patterns because of the shared contexts and because of some shared beliefs.

This chapter will examine the influence these societal conditions and values have on relating styles in general. Relationships, in general, receive less focused attention and concern than other matters in American society. Social conditions have a significant impact on life in America. It will be necessary to deal with various social issues separately although they exist in an interdependent frame each affecting and being affected by the others.

Family and Community

In previous times American culture set the stage for relation. Important institutions implicitly included relations with others. Circumstances have changed permitting a difference in the number of relations that develop and the ways people relate today.

The institution of the family was a vibrant force in society. Extended families built relationships between generations because of interdependent roles played by family members. Extended families

1

provided opportunities for large numbers of possible relationships with cousins, uncles, aunts, and grandparents. Siblings and other relatives lived in close proximity most, if not all, of their lives.

Family functions were much more encompassing including economic, educational, and social aspects. Families not only lived together but were employed in common tasks. In an economy based on production, the farm family depended upon a large number of family members in order to accomplish the strenuous planting, reaping, and other tasks. Affective ties followed from the close working conditions. Because of continued association, family members developed and maintained interests in the same things.

In an econcomy based on consumption families today do not have the same interdependent roles. Many responsibilities previously assumed by the family now have been assumed by non-personal institutions in society. For example, the family no longer has entire responsibility for social and moral development of the children. As many public arguments attest the impersonal institution of the school is expected to pass on moral values. It is also the obligation of the school to direct medical care, i.e. innoculations; proper nutrition, i.e. lunch program; recreation, i.e. athletics. It is even the responsibility of the school to direct socialization in such mundane areas as acquisition of proper social etiquette. In fact, as many educators imply, families are not capable of "teaching" these things, supporting, therefore, the raison d'être.

Family members don't rely on each other as they used to. One or two family members have been delegated the economic responsibilities; the others are given no responsibility in these or other household matters, and thus have no recognized place of importance in the family. It is not surprising that, in the manner of a self-fulfilling prophecy, these members begin to act irresponsibly.

Previously children learned trades by participating in "family occupations." Apprenticeship, a common form of education, involved the individual learner in all features of work. The apprentice was a part of the master tradesman's community, often residing in the master's house. Education for a trade was not disconnected from education as a family and community member. Vocational schools today are often segregated from the "real world of work" and the community. This disconnection of work from meaning in the community is artificial and may be alienating. In the past, working and learning together in a community setting created a strong sense of cohesion and meaning for life.

Education and socialization were family and community concerns. Values were passed more directly from generation to generation with little exposure to conflicting values. People were constantly exposed to familiar others with similar values and concerns. Common values led to greater sense of unity. There was firmer ground on which to build friendships.

Today the structure of society does not help relations develop. Rather it tends to discourage relations. The family is diminished so that the nuclear family, and lately, the one parent family are common forms. Children grow up not knowing their relatives or only dutifully visiting cousins, grandparents, and even parents at the required once a year holiday gathering.

In the past, small neighborhoods were closely knit communities similar to families, for they had common interests and acted interdependently. Institutions such as community church and small community schools furnished a stage for relations to develop. People were exposed to the same individuals year after year. They became familiar with each other's habits, values, beliefs. There was a consistency in their associations, thus allowing relationships to form.

Small community run churches, schools, and small businesses have been exchanged for large, complex, centralized, and impersonal institutions which have taken away the sense of connection. Influence between community members is far less prevalent; almost absent in large urban centers. In the past children attended small schools in which they learned from each other and from a teacher who was a member of, and strongly influenced by, the community. Today the child is bused, sometimes long distances, to the large brick building staffed with experts who claim to know children better than parents. The sense of influence one had with one's children is lost and interdependent family needs and roles are also lost.

The small business establishments, where discussions extended from politics to cooking tips, were an integral part of community life. Theses have been discarded in the large department-style store, where employees change with the season and personal concern and contact are almost non-existent. Institutions of extended family, small community schools, businesses, and churches are found only in a few rural settings. The absence of these personalized institutions causes a major difference in the cultural climate and thus in the possibilities for relationship formation.

Values and Social Conditions in America

Several American values and behaviors tend to discourage the formation of relationships. Individualism, competition, economic advancement, hierachies and mobility create attitudes and behaviors which work against relations. These values are held by the adult American population and it is significant to note that children are socialized in early life to develop these attitudes. The kinds of values taught children intentionally and unintentionally are indicative of the values held by adults and the values that will be held by future adults.

Individualism

Individualism is a counter-force to relationship formation, yet it is a prominent American value. It has its roots in Calvinism and the Protestant ethic. The Calvinist doctrine, brought from Europe to New England in early seventeenth century, taught that all social relations, even brotherly love, were of no consequence for salvation, the ultimate goal for life. These teachings fostered an attitude of individualism by declaring that each individual was entirely and only responsible for himself or herself. Calvinism declared that trust should only be placed in God and in fact, directly discouraged relations with others with "warnings against any trust in the aid of friendship of men" (Weber, p. 106, 1958). Individualism is still both a fact and an ideal in American life, publicly worshipped (Whyte, p. 5, 1956).

The Protestant ethic puts salvation in the hands of each individual, through hard work, thrift and the competitive struggle. The philosophy of social Darwinism theorizes that the human species evolves naturally through the competitive struggle which allows the strongest to surface by destruction of the weakest. Individuals are pitted against each other in this struggle to be the best. Social Darwinism came to this country after individualism had already become a national tradition but it lent theoretical weight to individualism and increased in prominence (Hofstadter, p. 50, 1944).

Individualism has been a useful concept in American progress by permitting each person to develop to his or her greatest potential. Yet individualism, pushed to excess, deters formation of relations for it forces one to be a pillar of self-sustained strength with no need or desire to relate. Although individualism allows one to become more independent, self-reliant, and self-directed, it also makes one more

isolated, alone, and afraid. It is important to maintain a careful balance on the continuum between dependence and individualism.

In the past few decades individualism has taken a new direction. There has been an increase in self-concern, egocentrism, and narcissism. This trend seems to have its roots in several aspects of recent history. The era of permissive child-rearing practices has permitted a continuation into adulthood of what Piaget had labelled egocentric behavior, a part of the development of the young child. This permissiveness allows the child to be the center of his small universe with all requests fulfilled without question. This early experience creates a reality which is carried into adult life. The adult then, attempts to continue behaving in the same manner. Also prolonged adolescence into the decade of the twenties, with continued schooling has allowed a disregard for social responsibility.

Children are strongly socialized in individualistic behavior. In particular, young men, are encouraged to be self-reliant. In this age of affluence, everyone has his or her own room, own toys, own television. Sharing is a thing of the past.

In addition to these forces, the growing presence of "pop psychology" attempts to give scientific support to selfishness. Both the self-help books and jargon abound. People are "looking out for number one" and "doing their own thing" and have no time for others. A consciousness of personal growth does not have to discourage relations; when presented like this it too often does..

Competition

Competition is an American way of life. It is predominant in work and extends into all areas including leisure activities. Children learn competitive behavior early in life. By the time they reach adulthood they are well versed, often getting ahead at the expense of others. In their earliest years they are conditioned to be competitive through parental rewards for winning. They learn through imitation of other children and adults. They learn through verbal teachings from parents, teachers, and television. Competition through practice permits children to become proficient.

Much of a child's life is spent in school. The school is an enormously competitive arena. There is competition for attention of the teacher and other students but more prevalent is the constant competition for grades, a system overtly promoted by the adult population. The application of the ubiquitous normal curve in schools

creates competition. The statistically predetermined criteria of success, the normal curve, ensures that some students fail while only a few do well. There are, of course, only benefits for those who win (or do well). Children learn quickly and it isn't long before they realize that it is easier to be rewarded for doing excellently by lowering the standards of the normal curve. By making others fail, or fail more completely, it is easier for the child to appear as if he or she is doing excellent work. This kind of competition starts in grade school and continues throughout high school and college where the rewards appear greater and greater and therefore the ferociousness of competition increases.

The extreme impact of competition is found in play where concern for others, fair play, and honesty succumb to the need to win. Hurting opponents verbally, or by covert physical attacks, are an accepted means of advancing the standing of one's own team. At youngsters' games, the parent/spectators are often much more competitive in their verbal insults than the children who are playing. These little athletes learn from the parent/spectators' comments that winning is far more important than other aspects of sports. These youngsters also have many sports heroes (who are often devastating competitors) to emulate. Even the non-athletic games our society plays ultimately have one winner and several losers. In fact it is possible to play at activities where no one loses but these are uncommon means of entertainment in American society. There is a significant impact and carry-over from competitive sports and play activities to work and social milieus.

Contrary to the American faith in the productive value of competition it is only one strategy to promote excellence. Studies done by Urie Bronfenbrenner in the Soviet Union point out a push for excellence through group competition which, instead of pitting person against person, fosters intergroup cooperation. Children in all phases of their schooling help and encourage each other to improve. Helping others is in the best interest of the group and the individual (Bronfenbrenner, p. 50, 1970). This kind of early childhood training carries over into the value system of Soviet adult society. Fostering cooperative behavior in American children, through structured activities and verbal sanctions would increase cooperative behavior for the future adult society as well. Recent studies of Japanese management also point to the value of intergroup cooperation (Ouchi, 1981). Although competition has been a salient factor in American progress, it appears to have become a force that separates people.

Capitalism and Economic Advancement

Another philosophy which is inimical to relationship formation is that of capitalism. Capitalistic economic activity has been a means to improve the standard of living for many people. Its worth has been enormous but too often today it is a goal in itself. The need for economic advancement leads to the "kill or be killed" attitude. Individuals focus on creating losing situations for others to increase winning situations for themselves.

The movement of Protestantism parallels the movement of capitalism. Both tended to push toward individualism and away from relation. In addition "in both spheres there is a manifest decline of custom and tradition and a general disengagement of purpose from the context of community" (Nisbet, p. 94, 1962). The sense of purpose of community is adumbrated by attention to economic gains.

Work, as a means, has been replaced by work, as an end in itself. According to Maier (1973), work is valued as a "primary justification for man's existence" (p. 415). The Protestant ethic, present here again, encourages dedication to work. Behavior in accordance with the Protestant ethic is not uncommon. Studies indicate this behavior is prominent and has been labelled as a personality type. The Protestant ethic personality places positive value on hard and steady work, ambition and self control; negative value is attributed to comfortable and exciting life, pleasure and equality (Merrens and Garrett, p. 360-4, 1978).

Another economic attitude which works against relation is the significance ascribed to money. For some people, the accumulation of capital becomes the purpose for work. One's economic standing has come to represent one's inherent value thus the size and contents of one's house are a means of social status in our society. Expensive pursuits may be engaged in for the purpose of displaying one's social status more than for the pleasure derived. Note vacationers so affixed to picture-taking that they miss experiencing the new surroundings in their concentration for recording the experience for later display.

With this kind of behavior people attempt to identify with objects rather than "subjects." Things are substituted for people. If the goal in life is to increase one's wealth and social standing, relationships take second place. In fact, relationships may curtail movement toward this goal and thus have no place at all in climbing the economic ladder of life.

The economic structure of American society creates still another detriment to developing relations: inequality. The work environment is organized in a hierarchical fashion to maximize the social distance between those at the top and those at the bottom. This acts as a method for management control, makes for dominant/subordinate positions, and ascribes a high status to those at the top (Bowles and Gintus, p. 83, 1976). The hierarchical structure also acts to distance workers on different levels of the hierarchy. In addition, the fragmenting of jobs and responsibilities prevents the development of coalitions even between the workers themselves. Possible associations are truncated by the structure of the work place. A major outcome of this hierarchical structure is to create inequality and bolster the economic and social status of a few, similar to the theory of social Darwinism.

Experiential learning about inequality is not only present in the world of work. Children are socialized early to their proper positions in society. Children, quite aware of their social standings, are constantly reminded of their positions by the paths they find open to them. Schools enforce the status differences. Schools have a hierarchical structure much the same as business. In fact, "the structure of educational experience is admirably suited to nurturing attitudes and behavior consonant with participation in the hierarchical labor force" (Bowles and Gintus, p. 9, 1976). The kinds of behaviors rewarded in schools are those most appropriate in the work environment. Children are schooled in inequality. The dominant/subordinate orientation learned in schools is not easily dismissed in later life and thus relation formation is hindered.

Corporate Structure

The hierarchical structure and competitive nature of the work environment produce conflicts between bosses and subordinates and between numerous factions of the organization. According to Mangam "conflicts are not confined industrial organizations." They are found, for example, in universities, where "schools, departments, and facilities 'compete' for resources...." Other work seetings are cited as replete with tensions and possibly some tolerance (Mangam, p. 212, 1981).

Those in the corporate arena need the solace that relationships can afford. According to Oliver it is not only the corporate executive who can be overwhelmed by the stresses of corporate life. Schools, as well as work settings, are corporate organizations which drain a person's

resources. The stresses in these organizations are not easily offset for there are few avenues for renewal. As Oliver points out, the relations available do not always meet the needs. "...relatively transient albeit relationships do not have the force to balance the pressure of a corporate identity. The nuclear family is too fragile and emotionally charged to deal with the competency requirements of corporate settings - in schools, jobs, etc." (Oliver, p. 6, 1976).

There is a need for a broader base of relationships to overcome the stresses of corporate life. Oliver suggests the intentional community where individuals are committed to each other in more than a superficial manner. The nuclear family today is sometimes overwhelmed by the needs of its member. Additional strong relationships can disperse the strain, particularly in times of excessive stress. Unlike some might suggest, friendships can support not dilute family relationships.

Mobility

Another deterrent to relationship formation is mobility. Residential moves are usually the result of occupational directives. The family relocates to continue progression up the ladder or to celebrate advancement by purchasing a bigger home to indicate the improved status of the family moving up. Thus it is economics and status which dictate one's life decisions. Friends and families are separated by moving. The option of remaining in the more familiar atmosphere, with people one knows, at the cost of remaining at the present income level, is typically not even seen as an option.

The ease and prevalence of nomadic behavior in this society decreases the desire to develop strong bonds, because the inevitable breaking of these ties is painful. It is difficult to make friends with only a few years in one location. Mobility increases our skills at disconnection for proficiency usually comes with practice.

Avoidance of Relation

Although American values tend to inhibit the formation of relationships, Americans do hold an ideal of strong connections with others. Affection, support, affirmation, and all subsequent outcomes of relationships are sought through quicker, more impersonal means. The mushrooming enterprises of support groups, singles groups, and

diversification of psychotherapeutic styles and purposes seem to indicate a need.

Americans seem to be looking for the rewards of relationships. They just don't know exactly what they want or how to find it. Some Americans seek relief from loneliness and isolation in pseudo-solutions which are directed at the symptoms and not the cause of problems. These pseudo-solutions may take the form of communes, encounter groups, trial marriages, and the like, where the quantity of relations is often substituted for the quality. Short term connections are wrongly considered to have the same attributes of relationships with history and future. These pseudo-solutions, in fact, perpetuate the dis-ease they seek to overcome.

The avoidance of making basic connections and commitments and avoidance of intimacy promote detachment. Individual concerns and self-centered life styles may cause feelings of isolation and lack of identity. This encourages mobility and objectification of others creating a self-sustaining cycle. Continuing contact with significant others provides the avenues for development of stability and a sense of identity so crucial in this rapidly changing world (Kirkpatrick, p. 6, 1975).

The structure of today's society appears to be fostering a sense of anxiety and rootlessness. In our culture "...with its cherished values of individual self-reliance and self-sufficiency, surrounded by relations which become ever more impersonal...there is a rising tendency, even among 'normal' elements of the population toward increased feelings of aloneness and insecurity" (Nisbet, p. 17-18, 1962). The historical structures which gave a sense of connection and meaning have been replaced by the impersonal and alienating.

It seems that social and geographic mobility is creating a character structure (previously considered a character disorder) which displays itself in "shallow, transitory objective relations with little subjective feeling" (Bellak, p. 417-8, 1963). In the long run this results in a sense of loneliness and lack of belonging.

Harry Stack Sullivan, who considered the development of personality dependent on interpersonal relations, suggests that personality disorders are a manifestation of our social instability. The very structure of our society today, tends to produce disconnection and neurosis, and to prohibit adjustment (Nisbet, p. 18, 1962).

William Sadler, who has written about friendship and love, claims that alienation, cynicism, and despair are the direct result of lack of friendships and the resultant loneliness (p. 209, 1970). Pseudo-solutions of temporary connections only camouflage, they do not

provide real solutions which call for in-depth, meaningful relationships. People need to be connected to be able to really know other people.

These various contextual and attitudinal circumstances, make relating difficult and create an unstable position for friendship in America today. As has been shown these changes are not always overt or contented with easily. Another important obstacle in the path to increased relating is the absence of sanctions. Friendship has very few sanctions in this society, but a counter-part, marriage, has many. A brief look at social sanctions prescribed for marriage may elucidate the difficulties encountered by the dirth of like sanctions for friendship.

Marriage: A Comparison

Some relationships are given legal and spiritual sanction but friendship has no such helpful support. Although, as a relationship, friendship allows for the much praised ideal, of freedom, as well as affective and psychological rewards, it is not recognized as a viable relationship. Jacqueline Wiseman's empirical study of friendship states this issue clearly. "The friendship bond is exceedingly fragile when compared with other, more institutionalized relationships such as marriage" (p. 191, 1986).

Marriage is a strongly supported relationship, verbally and legally in the United States. Marriage is institutionalized. It has existed both legally and in religious contexts and has extensive historical roots. This institutionalization provides the basis for its continuation.

Marriage is sanctioned also by a number of overt actions. A ceremony serves to announce the commencement of a concrete relationship. Newspaper announcements and legal certificates of marriage are social and legal statements which enforce compliance with various expected behaviors. The visible manifestations of marriage are themselves important for this institution; the sharing of living space and other household items, the presence of a wedding ring, the verbal statement of role relationships as wife and husband.

If there are difficulties that arise within the marriage there are external means of arbitration. If one or both of the marriage partners feels a dissatisfaction in an aspect of the relationship an appeal can be made to a non-participant. A marriage counselor, a lawyer, and judge, all have knowledge, and social titles for intervening. Thus the "legitimate" recourse for inappropriate actions within marriage are institutionalized.

Overt sanctions are part of the institutionalization of marriage in the United States and are largely responsible for its continuation. None of these kinds of sanctions exist for friendship in this country. Most assuredly one reason is Americans don't feel that friendship deserves a place of distinction. Yet friendship is a relationship thoroughly worthy of support. Friendship does receive considerable sanctions in some other cultures (Brain, p. 19, 1976; Firth, p. 109 1967; Cohen, p. 351, 1961; Paine, p. 147, 1974).

Friendship behavior is not taught directly or presented through subtle socialization methods in this country. Little children learn about adult behavior through play. They play house, taking the role of wife, husband, mother, or father, but they do not copy adult models and play friends. Marriage is something that almost every American boy and girl thinks about and plans for. It is a relationship most parents prod their children towards. It is seen as the adult mode of life and, in fact, is a major rite of passage into adulthood.

Adolescents learn through role play situations where they take on behaviors of certain roles without necessarily taking the names and costumes of such roles. Again adolescents take on the roles of spouses in their dating and courtship behaviors. They do not role play friends; some such roles are not permitted. Mixed sex associations are automatically labelled "dating behavior." This is not to say that children and adolescents do not have friends but that they do not have models or chances at acting out the roles of friends. Thus it is understandable that they have trouble relating as adults with no socialization, little practice and few models.

As with other things that require learning, adults are not likely to pick up the ability to relate as friends once they have matured. An adult's concern is focused on adult things which in American society surely does not include the "childish" concept of friendship. The attention of the adult is directed at the singular adult relationship, marriage. As the acme of American relationships, it unfortunately excludes other strong relationships. This is, of course, not helpful to friendship formation.

Friends held previous to marriage are often discontinued upon marriage. Particularly women's friendships are terminated after marriage. Recent research suggests that particularly "women's intimacy needs may not be completely met by spouses" (Tschann, p. 79, 1988). Yet relationships outside of marriage are often perceived as undermining the exclusivity of marriage and therefore are discouraged. If, however, marriage is the only strong relationship that husband and wife have, it receives all the pressures from both of their lives. Sometimes this

creates a pressure cooker effect. Strong relationships outside of marriage, can serve to strengthen marriage by relieving some of the pressure on the marriage.

Marriage, as an institution, with all of its sanctions appears to be having increasing difficulty in present day society. It may well be that the strains of constant change are too much for marriage, one of the last close relationships available to adults in our society, to deal with alone. Increased friendships may be advantageous in sustaining marriage as well as for dispelling the alienating effects of our society.

Summary

Friendship, although a valuable relationship, exists in an alien environment. The structural make-up of this society provides little foundation for friendship. There are no social sanctions for friendship. There is no education for it; much of the American socialization process supports individualism and competition which work against friendship formation. Because of these factors, friendship is an unstable relationship within our society, tottering on a narrow ridge. Investigation and increased understanding of friendship will help put it on more sure footing and thus help provide the individual rewards and societal benefits which this relationship is capable of giving.

Chapter 2

Relational Types

To completely understand the fabric of friendship it is important to view the texture from various perspectives. Thus the social context and historical framework for friendship have been considered in the last chapter. Our indiscriminate use of the term tends to obfuscate the real boundaries and components of friendship. This chapter will explore a number of different types of relations; other cultures' more discriminating categorization of friendship; and significant philosophical discourses on friendship.

An investigation of friendship will here be restricted to relations between two people for although friendship may exist in various contexts be it large group or only two persons, a friendship is literally the connection between one person and another person and cannot be subsumed under one's association with a group. Relation possibilities can be divided into four major types: formal, social, personal, and kinship relations.

Types of Relations

Formal Relations

Within a formal relation the two individuals associate on the basis of roles. The roles, predetermined by title or position, are often socially imposed. The relation is defined by the roles. Any individual may be placed in either role and the formal relation may continue without undue difficulty. The formal relation between doctor and patient is an example. Any individual may be placed in either role (assuming equal ability to perform the role). Thus for the doctor, any *body* will do; for the patient any competent doctor will do.

Precedent has produced definite rules and regulations for each role within the relation and the individuals are clear about their respective positions and expected behaviors. There are definite boundaries to each role that are not crossed. The doctor asks the questions; the patient is the one who disrobes. The doctor is the one who directs and instructs; the patient listens and cooperates with

15

instructions. Such definite rules can be both a help and a hindrance. Transactions can be much quicker and more precise when the exchange of goods or services is the only issue. It also can prevent interaction not accepted under the rules of the role even though alteration of these roles might be beneficial on a particular occasion. In other words, formal relations become solidified and prevent variation to meet the changing situation.

The formal relation, then, is characterized by rules and regulations determined by particular roles. Impersonal interaction and existence of the relation is usually for business purposes only.

Social Relations

Social relations also have rules, many of which fall within the category of etiquette and sociability. The social relation also contains more personal elements than does the formal relation, which, in its strictest sense exists without any personal knowledge of the other at all. The social relation might exist between the small town grocer and his patrons whom he knows as individuals. He greets a customer out of compliance with social dictates and remarks about recent occurrences in her family because he knows her in a social manner. People may be more or less willing to engage in socializing behavior, to talk in social niceties, and to enjoy one another's company.

The degree of compliance to norms within the social relation varies proportionately to the degree of closeness (personal knowledge and concern) of the individuals. Neighbors commonly have a social relation. A variety of needs: social support, confirmation of identity, and simple enjoyment, can be obtained through social relations.

Personal Relations

Although there are some regulations that are present in personal relationships they are fewer in number than in formal and social relations. These requirements are socially imposed and are predominantly necessary for the two people to fit into the larger social framework. Within the confines of the personal relationships these regulations may well be disregarded and elements of role relations are absent. The personal relationship can be said to contain some norms which evolve through the development of the relation. These are

normative in the sense of setting a pattern or standard of behavior, so the two will know how to act with each other, yet they are not normative in the sense of being typical or average. These norms are personal to the two individuals within the relation. They can, like the socially imposed regulations, be waived with greater ease since approval for waiver is only needed from one individual who is personally involved in the relation.

The personal relation does not exist for the purpose of business affairs. Nor is it constrained by sociability requirements such as neighbors who must be nice to each other since they have to live next door to one another. To say that a personal relation exists for any particular purpose is somewhat contrary to its real nature, yet obviously the personal relationship does serve a purpose. The outcomes are of a more psychological nature and will be examined more fully later.

Kinship Relations

Roles and rules both exist in kinship. The role of mother carries with it some basic rules such as responsible behavior toward her children. Kinship may exist simultaneously with personal relationships such as with spouses. The title of husband or wife differentiates roles and thus indicates to some degree appropriate behavior toward the other.

In one sense kinship relations could be said to exist for the purpose of begetting and caring for offspring but, for example, second cousins do not associate for such a purpose, although they may well acknowledge their kinship and associate with one another. It could be said that these kinship connections do not serve a purpose at all and are simply a natural occurrence; that is, common ancestry, but then why do second cousins actually take time to visit one another? A sense of obligation, socially or familiarly imposed, often dictates the required behavior.

Comparing Relations

The distinctions between these four types of relations are not precise and varying types of relations may occur at varying times. A good example of the vagueness of boundaries is noted by Allan, who points out the difficulty of ascertaining certainty of distinctions even in

kinship relationships which perhaps seem the most definitive. Although we usually consider kin to be those who fit either the "social kinship" category (that is socially arranged; i.e. marriage) or the "natural kinship" category (through birth) the clarity of distinction becomes confused with regard to adopted children, step-parents, distant relatives, and in-laws. In addition, when interviewing numerous people Allan found that some people are treated as kin, without any belief in blood or marriage ties, and blood kin often do not associate in a kinship manner. So people behave as kin when they are not and do not behave as kin when they are. Allan thus designates kinship relations as "categorical" labels which simply serve the purpose of locating people in the social structure (Allan, p. 34, 1979).

Besides studying the issues of roles, rules, and purposes of relational types, other criteria influence relationships. The social context, the types of bonds, and the culture of the relation all provide some clarification of these different relations.

Social Context

"Relationships develop within a definite context," and this context must be perceived as influential in the development and functioning of the relationship (Andreyera and Gozman, p. 48, 1981). To the extent that the two people become involved in their respective roles and consequent behaviors, the social context even exerts control on the feelings these two have for each other. This is perhaps best understood by example.

In a courtroom a lawyer and judge, while court is in session, behave in a strictly formal manner using specific titles and following precise rules. They have a definite role relation and they do not deviate from legality or protocol. In the judge's chambers they still hold their respective role positions yet some formality may be dispensed. Lines of authority still exist and regulations indicate behavior.

On the golf course, the judge and lawyer may still acknowledge differences in position, "the judge tees off first," although they are likely to maintain a more social-type relation. In the lawyer's home, with their respective spouses, norms still exist; the judge may not jump up and down on the couch and throw things around the living room. If the lawyer and judge are completely alone, again a change in social context, they may engage in activity which otherwise they would not. They may use language which they wouldn't use "in front of the

ladies," or throw popcorn at one another in a moment of silliness. Thus a change in place and the presence or absence of others greatly influence what type of relation two people may have with each other.

Bonds

According to George McCall, the bonds that unite persons in relation are indicative of the kind of association that exists. McCall describes five different types of bonds: *ascription*, socially imposed roles; *commitment*, personally giving oneself to the responsibility of particular aspects of a relation with another, often in order to insure exchange of various rewards; *attachment*, involvement in another's life to the extent that the other actually becomes part of one's own identification of self; *investment*, giving of the scarce personal resources such as time and energy to the other; *reward dependability*, a means of securing exchange of social commodities (McCall, 1970).

According to McCall, bonds, like the relations in which they are found,

> usually blend and run together in most continuing relationships. Nevertheless they are distinct factors; they are present in different proportions in different relationships, and they often vary independently of one another....Individuals are most preoccupied with their attachments, but the societies they live in are most concerned with their ascriptions and commitments....People tend to make investments on the basis of their attachments, particularly in the early phases of relationships, in attempts to secure commitments from other parties as dependable sources of exchange rewards (McCall, p. 9-10, 1970).

Distinctions between relation types can be made on the basis of the type of bond present. The primary bond in formal relations in ascription, the bond most common in social relations is commitment, the bond most predominant in personal relations is attachment, and the bond distinguishing kinship is ascription.

Culture of the Relation

The actual behavior within the relation is a distinguishing feature of the kind of relation. Even with the more stringent formal relations there are general idiosyncratic behaviors peculiar to that particular relation. For example, Principal Smith may have only a formal relation with the various teachers in his school, yet Principal Smith may call Teacher Jones by his first name and vice versa, while Principal Smith may call Teacher Arnold only by his surname and vice versa. This type of particularistic behavior tends to develop because of certain instances in the evolution of the relation and is maintained mostly through precedent. As these school personnel maintain formal relations only and are thus role-related, with specified positions and behaviors, they are unlikely to change their historically developed behavior toward one another.

As relations become more informal this particularistic nature of the relation becomes larger. The private culture of the relation, as McCall labels it, becomes especially important in the personal relation where the two people begin to understand and explain things on the basis of their private interaction, such as explanation of present events through past experiences common only to the two.

Friendship as a Personal Relation

One of the reasons friendship has not been much investigated is the large dimension of private culture present in the relation. Because much of the relation is private, understanding, distinguishing, and describing it is difficult. Although the activity in the relation is not entirely unknown, the concealment of specifics makes comparison with other similar relations difficult and therefore hampers description and definition. The relation cannot be explained by ascribed roles and expected behaviors because the norms of the relation are determined privately by the two. The privacy, the concealment of specifics, is a major asset to the strength and personal nature of the relation.

According to this typology of relation, friendship could, in a broad sense, be found in the categories of either social or personal relations. In later chapters, friendship will be discussed predominantly as a personal relationship. Friendship, of course, can exist within the bounds of kinship as well but there are additional role-related behaviors expected of such a friendship.

Persons who always maintain a formal relation with one another would not call themselves friends although it is clear that individuals can take on a formal relation within a particular social context and in another context associate in the manner of the personal relation of friendship.

Friendship is a relation, unlike most other relations, that has no ultimate conclusion, no end result or product. Formal relations such as business relation exist for the purpose of production; teacher/student relation primarily exists to increase the learning and growth of the child; the therapist/client relation, policeman/citizen relation have specified purposes for existence. Friendship focuses on process, not content. It is the relation itself that is of the greatest value. Unlike formal relations, it is not product-oriented; it is not concerned with outcomes.

By narrowing the boundaries, friendship in the American culture can be seen more distinctly. In the few explorations of the area of friendship, the relation has been treated as distinct while in fact it varies across a large range of predominantly social and personal relations. In other cultures friendship's characteristics are more recognizable because of specific, often clearly designated divisions in friendship types.

Cross-Cultural Comparison

A cross-cultural comparison will help to illuminate some characteristics of friendship. A number of anthropologists have described the different types of friendship found in other cultures. It is possible, in examining other cultures, to see facets of friendship not so clearly visible in our own culture. The more overt, specific, and definitive expressions of friendship, the labelling of friends, and recognition of behaviors in other cultures distinguish friendship types.

A major difference between friendships in the United States and friendships that appear in some pre-industrial societies is the institutionalized aspect. Whereas in the U.S. friendship exists as a matter of whim, some cultures have established friendship as a major relation recognizing it through rites, ceremonies, and clearly stated expectations of behavior and obligation. In this kind of habitat, friendship is seen as a primary relation not as a secondary relation as is common in the U.S.

One anthropologist, Robert Brain, suggests that friendship in American culture exists only through vague bonds of sentiment, whereas other cultures attach rites and requirements to friendship making it more clear and stable. Brain points to clear distinctions between types of friendship with the Bangwa of the Cameroon mountains.

> The Bangwa, great adepts at friendship of every kind, recognize a clear difference between chosen or "achieved" friends, who are called "friends of the heart," and obligatory or "ascribed" friends, who are "friends of the road." A man's best friend, however, is a "friend of the road" since he is the one born nearest in time to himself (Brain, p. 108, 1976).

Firth gives another specific example of distinctive classes of friends in Tikopia, a Polynesian island of the Solomons. Bond friendship of the Tikopia is an institutionalized, life-long bond, "reinforced and expressed by reciprocal obligations, mutual trust and periodical exchange of gifts" (Firth, p. 108, 1967).

Non-bond friend-relations exist in Tikopia but the acknowledgement of another as a friend of this nature is a matter of courtesy. The general population of the Tikopian community is clearly aware of the spheres of the relations of each individual with all others. The bond relation in Tikopia is chosen, generally during early adulthood, and consists of an initial rite which signifies the bond. Obligations are not clearly defined in the bond relation except for periodic gift-exchanges. According to Firth the main purpose of bond-friendship in Tikopia is to provide a man "with a confident outside the immediate kinship circle, one on whom he can rely for aid against all else" (p. 110, 1967).

Cohen suggests that all societies develop a pre-disposition toward friendship relations. In an extensive cross-cultural study he has found four main categories of friendship each dependent on the type of society in which it is found. *Inalienable* friendship is institutionalized, entered ritually with clear duties and responsibilities, and cannot be withdrawn from. Such a friendship exists in a society which has close proximity of all members, extended families, and a highly integrated kin group. *Close* friendship has the similar emotional and social aspects of inalienable friendship but it is an informal relation without quasi-legal enforcement and can be broken at any time. Close

friendship is found within a society that has strong bonds of kinship but not a strong tie to the land allowing for greater mobility and severing of ties. *Causal* friendship is not recognized by the culture as a social category and has no duties, rights, or privileges, does not imply allegiance or affiliation, and has little social, material or economic sharing. This type of friendship evolves within a society where families are isolated from one another geographically and emotionally. *Expedient* friendship is based purely on the gain that can be made through the relation. Expedient friendship develops within a social structure which is focused on individual accumulation of wealth as an end in itself (Cohen, p. 314-317, 1961).

Friendships are not institutionalized in American society as are inalienable friendship and to a lesser degree, close friendship in some societies. An institutionalized relation has more clear roles and obligations, sanctions and considered worth (Cohen, p. 353, 1961; Ramsoy, p. 13, 1968). The mobility of American society largely prohibits the development of long lasting, deeper relations which need time and close association. Although institutionalization may somewhat curtail the variety of relations, it might in our society provide a much greater sanction for friendship which seems to have its footing eroded by changing times.

The anthropological perspective of DuBois looks more closely at the bonds of friendship. Here an exclusive friend is one who is prized for himself or herself. Exclusive friendship involves great intimacy, confidence and reciprocal responsibility and prohibits other important relations because of its intensity. A close friendship is "expressive and instrumental," and not exclusive. Both close and exclusive friendship involve life-long commitment. The casual friendship is contrasted as largely instrumental with no intent for an extended period of relation (DuBois, p. 19, 1974).

Exclusive and close friendship can only be maintained if intimacy is maintained; that is, the two must have sufficient contact and the continued growth of the individuals must be in the same general direction. The greater the divergence, the greater the strain on the relationship. The expectation of exclusive and close friendship then, is life-time duration yet its actuality is dependent on the development of the personality of the individuals and the amount of association (DuBois, p. 26, 1974).

Philosophical Considerations

Although anthropologists have been the primary investigators of friendship until the decade of the 70s the topic has been given serious consideration by several philosophers. One of the most commonly noted treaties on friendship is also one of the oldest. Aristotle was particularly concerned with the subject and discussion of it appears in several of his works. Aristotelian discourse on friendship is still as insightful and appropriate as it was two thousand years ago and it remains the most widely referenced elaboration on friendship.

DuBois's typology of friendship resembles that of Aristotle, who, like DuBois, poses three types of friendship basing the categories on motive. These categories, often indistinguishable from an external perspective, are based on usefulness, pleasure, or virtue. A *useful* friendship depends upon the good that can be accrued from the friend. A friendship of *pleasure* is dependent upon the enjoyment involved in the association. Both of these lack permanence for when the usefulness or pleasure is no longer present, friendship has no reason to exist. A friendship of *virtue* however, is not dependent upon conditions but on the good of the individuals and since goodness and virtue are things that last, such a friendship will last. A friendship built on virtue will be good for both people, for each partner is good and beneficial to the other (Aristotle, p. 218-226, 1962).

This elaboration of types of relations and some comparative examples of friendships in other cultures reveals a good deal about friendship. A closer examination of the intricacies of friendship in the next chapter will be necessary to truly understand the relationship.

Chapter 3

The Structural Framework of Friendship

Peter and Paul are good friends. Their friendship is comparable to the friendship between Michael and Mark. Basic underlying characteristics are common in all friendships but as they are not role relationships with specific requirements all friendships vary somewhat and are therefore hard to define. One individual's friendships with several people will be experienced as different and may show observable signs of this difference to an objective bystander.

This chapter will examine the structural framework of friendship, those basic underlying characteristics which all friendships have in common. Uniqueness, dyadic make-up, dynamic and voluntary aspects, and the entity of the relationship itself will be discussed in this chapter. The next chapter will explore conditions for initiating and continuing friendship and the phenomenological aspects which may vary to a degree dependent upon the individuals involved.

Friendship can be viewed within the scope of either a social relation (similar to Aristotle's friendships of usefulness or pleasure) or personal relation (similar to Aristotle's friendship of virtue). Friendships that fall within the field of social relations are not unimportant but they exist in great variety, from the friendly association of complete strangers to simple socializing. They could include friendly association of individuals who have known each other all their lives yet have not developed the strong bond present in friendship as a personal relationship.

As this chapter begins exploring friendship as a close personal relationship a working definition will be assumed. A good friendship is a strong bond relationship involving two persons who care for one another, feel a sense of commitment and sharing, and who experience the relationship as one of equality and reciprocity. This kind of association exists within the rubric of personal relationships where the bond is attachment and most of the norms imposed on the relationship are set by the two relating persons.

Dyadic Structure

Friendship is a dyadic relationship. It is the simplest form of relating yet dyadic interaction is complex. Georg Simmel has explained several important aspects unique to a dyadic relation. The dyadic relation is special because it is exclusive. Experiences shared exclusively by the two, even though perhaps trivial in nature, become, as Simmel states, a secret. A secret tends to provide cohesion for the dyad and exclude others adding an element of intimacy. It is not even necessary that this "secret" be unknown to those outside of the dyad, but only that it has not been shared by others in common experience (Simmel, p. 368-371, 1964).

The dyad is felt to be a unit from the inside. A friendship creates a mutual social reality developing its own private culture including common past experience, complementary styles and secrets. The two also develop their own unique set of behaviors and their own norms.

Within the actual encounter of the relationship, each person is confronted only by the other. This has several consequences. There is no refuge from the other in fulfilling responsibility. There is no one to hide behind or to seek allegiance from and no way to create a coalition of support for one's own belief. Everything must be decided consensually; there is no majority rule. There must be mutual definition of both individuals' ways of behaving. Both individuals, in a sense, have complete control over the existence of the relationship, because with withdrawal by either, the relationship no longer exists.

By adding a third party in the encounter, all these characteristics are altered. A third person detracts from the intensity of the relation itself.

Once a dyadic relation is entered there is no such thing as isolated behavior (Wilmot, p. 81, 1975). While relating everything is done in relation to, or because of, the other and much may be done in reference to the other outside the relation. This is because the bond of attachment, as defined by McCall, involves a portion of self-identification through relation with the other.

A dyad provides the best forum for communication. "Two may talk and one may listen but three cannot take part in a conversation of the most sincere and searching sort" (Emerson, p. 172, 1969). This is because in a dyad the channel is direct although it is not a simple linear and one way event. A message is sent, then interpreted by the other and a response given. In communication of a transactional nature,

each person influences and is influenced by the other (Wilmot, p. 9, 1975).

The ways of being within the relation are unique to the two. In friendship, the deviation from the public norms may make the relationship more intimate. According to Suttles, deviations may also develop as if the two are "partners in crime," where friends have a mutual interest in preserving the private morality expressly because it is personal (Suttles, p. 199, 1970). Kurth states that acting outside the norms of propriety may be more revealing of one's innermost being (Kurth, p. 161, 1970). Revealing of one's innermost being, or what could be called self-disclosure, by one friend has a tendency to encourage revealing or self-disclosure by the other. Jourard discovered that self-disclosure begets self-disclosure (p.14, 1971). Disclosure tends to escalate through the reciprocal action it produces and thus the amount and intensity of personal information revealed is increased, and the relationship becomes more intimate.

Friendships do exist in non-dyadic situations. Persons can and do associate with more than one friend at a time. A community of friends is possible, though Emerson and others seem to feel one friendship is sufficiently taxing to prevent simultaneous friendship. Certainly simultaneous interaction between more than one friend will be much more difficult than in dyadic encounter. Hartmann explains well the difference between dyadic relating and triadic relating:

> ...love for him in the dyad creates an ethical situation
> of a special kind, an intimate, absolutely reciprocal
> union between two human beings. A third person
> requires again a new and equally special commitment.
> Distributed among several, love loses its personal
> character...(p. 230, 1932).

A distinctive relationship continues to exist while relating goes on with others outside that particular friendship. Additional relations, however, complicate associations through increased numbers of persons needing attention.

The Unique Nature

Each friendship is unique. This is largely due to the fact that it is not an institutionalized category of behavior. The relationship is

built by the two persons themselves who meet and together develop a relationship which is mutually satisfying. The relationship is therefore, one of a kind. The roles and rules are personally and cooperatively imposed. The relationship is immediately dependent on the two persons involved. A change of one of the two people makes another entirely unique relation.

There are no externally prescribed roles. Expectations of what this friend ought to be are found only within this relationship. According to Blom

> Friends and friendships are definitely relational phenomena. They do not refer to categories of social persons but to a type of relationship....They furthermore refer to personal or particularistic relationships because it is impossible to assign meaning to their usage without specifying the particular persons involved as opposed to the "impersonal: status relation, such as buyer/seller, actor/audience, etc." (p. 4-5, 1969).

The lack of easily applied personal and dyadic role obligations means that each relationship may set up its own system (Albert and Brigante, p. 43, 1962). Each dyadic personal relationship is, in fact, obliged to set up its own system of relating.

Because friendship is not a category with categorical requirements, it tends to allow one to be more individual, self-assertive, and self-possessed. A friend is confronted only by one other in a friendship. One's feelings and needs are not subsumed under the feelings of a group.

Friendship is the harbinger of free relationships (Parson, p. 233, 1915). It permits what other role relations would curtail. The "self-governing" aspect of the relationship permits personal needs to be met in the most appropriate way. Albert and Brigante conclude that friendship outgrows the range and depth of conventional roles and thrives in less institutionalized settings; it has non-specific, non-social determinants for what is adequate as a relationship for each person (Albert and Brigante, p. 43, 1962). Individual identity is supported in a relationship which develops its own morality and special world view. According to Suttles friends deviate from "social dictates" to be more what they themselves really are (p. 116, 1970). It is the acceptance within friendship which allows and encourages friends to disclose more

of their personal lives. The deviations from normal social behavior to uniquely personal ways of being help make each friendship unique.

The Dynamic Nature

One of the difficulties with perceiving how friendships develop is they belie typical developmental sequences. According to Duck and Sants "relationships are processes" that are not always consciously thought through (p. 27, 1983). Yet friends do think about their relationships, how they are relating, and they review the behaviors of their partners and try to make sense of them.

Friendship is dynamic. It involves action: even though the two persons may be quiet, the relationship is still vibrant, alive. The friendship is active during periods of separation of the two individuals as well as during times of personal contact. This dynamic of friendship is on a horizontal rather than a vertical axis. That is, it cannot be visualized as growing or dying but as constantly changing. The movement is continuous but the velocity is variable. As Greeley explains it

> There are...dramatic turning points in the friendship relationship, times of great transitional crises when a friendship either moves ahead rapidly to a new kind of joy and delight or when it begins to fall apart....But if there are decisive turning points in any friendship, it does not follow that progress in friendship is rapid. In many cases, movement between the dramatic leaps can be agonizingly slow, almost so slow as to be invisible (p. 131, 1971).

Friendship is not always full of great dynamic interplays. Persons learn how to deal with one another and they feel that particular issues are under control only to become aware of the need to learn "how to" in regards to these issues all over again. Apparent learning may not have lasting value because both the relationship and the friends themselves continue to change and constant readjustment is necessary.

Temporality

The importance of the social context in which relationships are embedded has been noted. Another important context is time. People expect their "relationships to grow" over time and yet they also assume some "continuity over time" (Duck and Sants, p. 29, 1983).
According to Duck and Miell

> Relationship development is a complex of many independent features, both cognitive and social, involving growth and knowledge about one another, the growth of liking, growth of intimacy (both knowledge and behaviour), growth of commitment, and a variety of other things (including alterations in the way in which partners *perceive the relationship*) ...[it is not simple] linearity of progress....The growth of liking, for example, includes not only an increase in its intensity but also changes in its form, both in the forms of its feelings and in the forms of its expression as well as in the form of the cues that stimulate or evoke it (Duck and Miell, p. 234, 1985).

People continually analyze their friendships and this influences the future course of friendship (Duck and Miell, p. 239, 1985). Consideration and analysis of friends and friendships is not always specific or intentionally directed. Often it is based on a need to understand.

Phillips and Metzger speak of negotiation and building contracts as a stage of friendship allowing for security and stability (p. 403, 1976). But friendship does not relax into stability of specific stages and friendship is not built on dependable definitions like contracts; at least not in American culture as a whole. There is no plateau where footing is secure. Although a modicum of stability is reached, friendship remains a dynamic, ever changing relationship. This is in part due to the fact that friendship is neither contractual nor institutionalized. "In order to endure, friendship must constantly be remade, renewed and deepened like life itself" (Lepp, p. 115, 1966). To find a place where the friendship is finally solid is to accept the status quo and because the two individuals, who are the relationship, continue to change, the relationship must at least keep up with the persons or it will not survive.

People do not grow in friendship as one grows to physical maturity, leaving some steps behind as new steps are obtained. Friendship remains a precarious association. Although a sense of connectedness and commitment is reached after a time, the dynamic relationship remains in constant flux.

Interdependent Characteristics

Friendship development includes an internalized feedback loop. Acquainting individuals regulate their behavior to influence relationship formation and continually analyze the emerging relationship (Duck and Miell, p. 239, 1985). Much of relationship development happens "all in the mind" according to Duck and as people begin to realize they are "in a relationship" perceptions and behaviors change (Duck, p. 42, 1988). An interdependence of various relationship proprieties influence the course of the emerging relationship which may shift in "degree" or "symmetry" over time (Kelley, Berscheid, Christensen, Harvey, Huston, Levinger, McClintock, Peplau, and Peterson, p. 38, 1983).

The complexity of the interdependent characteristics of relationships are noted by Hinde. "The behavioural and affective/cognitive aspects of interpersonal relationships are almost inextricably intertwined" (p. 2, 1981). He goes on to state that the "dialectic" of relations influences the nature of individuals, and individuals influence the relations they enter (p. 5, 1981).

Voluntary Association

Friendship is a voluntary association. Other associations are not the result of complete choice in initiation or continuation as friendship is. One has very little choice as to who will be one's teachers, associates at work, caretakers in the hospital, parents and siblings. There is, of course, *some* degree of choice in initiating such relationships except with regard to kin. It is external demands which make these relations different from the voluntary aspect of friendship. Association with certain persons, for example, in a job situation, is externally controlled by the need for money.

Friendship does not have these external controls. Any matter of external control over friendship, such as coercion by one partner or an outsider to the relationship, tends to negate the relationship.

Friendship must be a matter of desire; coercion can not create real friendship.

Friendship in American society is conceived and maintained as solely volitional. It has not become an institution in the American culture as a whole as has, for example, marriage. In the sense of friendship being an association which includes habituated actions, it is institutionalized "in nucleo." But for an association to become an institution of society rather than simply that of the dyad itself, the historical development needs to be extended, and routinization of the shared activities allowed to "thicken and harden" through transmission of these typifications to succeeding generations (Berger and Luckman, p. 57-9, 1967). It is common typification of the institution of marriage, for example, that the couple lives together. This is considered normal behavior in marriage, partly because this typification has been practiced for centuries. Such typifications do not occur in American friendships.

Friendships are wholly individualized and the specifics of rights and obligations within friendship are not generalizable. Friendship is characterized by its voluntary aspect.

The Entity of the Relationship

A friendly relation is constituted solely by the two persons, whereas a friendship has three component parts, the two persons and the entity of the relationship itself. The relationship is completely dependent on the two persons for its existence. If one member of the dyad withdraws there are no longer three components, only the two persons, no relationship. James and Savary describe this third component as the third self of friendship. It emerges only in the closest of friendships displaying some qualities of each friend and a uniqueness of its own (James and Savary, p. 43, 1976). A similar description of relationships is given by Duck and Miell who describe "emergent properties [of a relationship which] are of neither individual alone but which eventuate from their relationship and interaction..." (p. 229, 1985).

In a manner of speaking, the two persons are dependent on the relationship for their life as it is now experienced within the relationship. This is most clear in an encounter between the two persons and much less obvious when the two are not directly associating. Direct associating could take the form of face-to-face

interaction or letters, telephoning, or relating via a third person.

Friendship has an exterior appearance. The uniqueness of each relationship tends to defy definite structured character, but can be perceived from the outside as an entity.

Two persons who associate consistently in particular situations are seen as a unit, that is to say, these two are typified as a unit. Thereafter, when they are seen separately "the missing part" of the unit creates a conspicuous absence. Especially children's relationships are labeled "the twins," or "Mutt and Jeff," a conceptual unit. Outsiders view the relationship as a performing team (Denzin, p. 88, 1970). As adults are more likely to act independently and be affronted when not perceived as independent, labeling adult friends as a unit is less common.

The internal aspects of this unit are more profound than the external ones. Denzin suggests that "because relationships take on a life of their own, each member feels obligated to sustain that moral order to some degree on all occasions public or private" (p. 82, 1970). Those in the relationship feel the unit's presence in private association and public with or without the presence of the other, if the situation is generally met by the two together. As Davis states:

> An intimate relation is a living thing insofar as it becomes a distinguishable, self-maintaining unit that drags around its occasionally unwilling creators in order to sustain its own existence and that causes them to suffer great agony should it suddenly be wrenched apart. Whatever instinctual, emotional or rational considerations induce a pair of individuals to procreate an intimate relation, its processes shortly acquire an inertia or structure of their own apart from the motivating force (Davis, p. 285, 1973).

The extent to which this separate entity lives is tested by time and distance. Friendship, unlike friendly relations, involves an attitude, not just the activity of association. Friends separated by time and space may still conceive of this entity, even without the activity of association. The relationship therefore doesn't need to be experienced to exist. Thus a *friend in mind* is a relationship with considerable impact.

Simmel seems to contest this position. He states quite clearly that in a dyad there is no super-personal life, there are only the two confronted by each other. But as Simmel explains elsewhere,

faithfulness is a conspicuous force acting as "the inertia" to preserve the association itself, beyond any logical or causal factors. Thus it would seem as if the relation had grown beyond two people confronted only by themselves as Simmel notes earlier (Simmel, p. 123, 380-1, 1964).

Buber views the place of meeting between the people as the "sphere of the interhuman," which goes beyond the two individuals themselves. Maurice Friedman's introduction to Buber's *Knowledge of man* explains it aptly.

> when two individuals "happen" to each other, then there is an essential remainder which is common to them, but which reaches out beyond the special sphere of each. That remainder is the basic reality, the "sphere of the between" (Buber, p. 17, 1965a).

This "sphere" isn't other than the friends themselves but it is that part of them which extends outward toward the other. It is this, according to Buber which permits dialogue, true meeting, to occur.

It is this sphere of the interhuman, or as it is referred to here the entity of the relationship, which can provide friendship with a sense of continuance. This entity needs the careful attention of the two friends if it is to be preserved and nourished. It is this entity which is responsible for making a friendship much more than a friendly relation and to a great degree, it is this entity which is responsible for many of the rewarding features of friendship.

Friends relate within a dyadic framework. Although each friendship is unique unto itself, there are common charateristics. American friendship is a voluntary relationship. As a dynamic, ever changing relationship it develops, after some time, a third entity, that of the relationship itself. Though the structural components discussed here are common to all friendship; those commonalities do not make the friendship any less complex.

Chapter 4

Components of Friendship

Friendship does not exist in a vacuum. Friendship, as an entity, needs life supporting materials. Many of these materials are found in the two individuals who form the relationships, and there is some dependence on the social environment. In order for the seed of friendship to sprout, take root, grow, and flower there are a number of variables necessary.

The last chapter discussed the structural framework of friendship. This chapter will explore the necessary pre-requisites for friendship, human qualities of value, conditions essential for the development and continuation, and phenomenological aspects. Although the attributes described here are essential to a strong, lasting friendship because individuals' needs and expectations of friendship vary, these attributes may not be found in all relationships labeled friendship.

Research on Proximity

Psychologists and sociologists who have studied attraction, liking, and friendships have indicated that proximity is a salient factor in friendship formation. According to Berscheid and Walster, experts on interpersonal attraction, the simplest way to state the evidence is "other things being equal, the closer two individuals are located geographically, the more likely it is that they will be attracted to each other" (p. 46, 1969). They base this conclusion on data acquired through their own research and that of a number of others in the field. Thus one will be attracted to those next door first, and will be less likely to be attracted to those living a few doors away and will be attracted inversely with distance. The qualifying statement "other things being equal" poses a problem for making viable conclusions from the data. All things are not equal when talking about friendships nor can they be measured to determine degrees of inequality.

Although the data on attraction and liking brings to light some interesting areas of human behavior, it sometimes has clouded the issues of friendship. One of the major reasons for the erroneous statement that friendship is most controlled by issues of proximity is that friendship is not typically well defined. The term has been used in

35

its loosest form, meaning any type of friendship in social, personal, or even formal relations. Relationship studies done by Berscheid and Walster and others initially focused attention on issues such as sociometric choices and group membership. Results of data collected were only afterwards (sometimes by the researchers themselves and sometimes by others) generalized to the area of friends. When friendship is conceived as a personal relation, proximity is important for initial contact but quite marginal as an influential friendship characteristic.

Another difficulty in the conclusions made from studies on attraction and liking is the paucity of information about the percentages of people who live and work with each other (positive proximity), but do not associate as friends except for the minimum required by social etiquette.

One pre-requisite condition for friendship formation indeed is proximity in the sense of the presence of the other in one's life. Proximity allows one to have first-hand information, verbal and experiential, when initiating relating thus minimizing the risk of rejection. Although proximity is a necessary condition it is far from a sufficient condition for formation of friendship as might sometimes appear to be indicated by the research on liking and attraction. There are several other pre-requisite conditions which also are necessary but not sufficient conditions for friendship formation.

Pre-requisite Conditions

One pre-requisite condition is willingness to make one's self available to the other. This implies the desire for association and a restricted amount of other external issues that might overshadow relating. For example if one is already overtaxed with relationships, or if relations are presently providing negative returns, one may not engage in any activities which are likely to make new associations.

The basic construction of the relation also depends directly on the individuals involved. A friendship requires two persons independent enough to function separately. This necessitates some strength of self, primarily through awareness, respect and acceptance of self. As the philosopher Martin Buber describes it, first there is a "'primal setting at a distance' and the second 'entering into relation'...[for]...one cannot stand in relation to something that is not perceived as contrasted and existing for itself" (Buber, p. 60, 62, 1965a).

People must be able to interact. Even in the initial processes of friendship, risk is a factor. An insecure person is likely to be fearful and not engage in conversation and opportunities which might lead to friendship. Likewise someone who has been recently hurt in an interpersonal encounter will hesitate. There must be a willingness to risk one's self-esteem if a relationship is to develop even in the beginning.

There are numerous personal attributes that philosophers have noted as necessary for developing and maintaining friendships. Philosophers appear to be concerned with ideal relations while social scientists are more concerned with observing the behavioral aspects of real friendships. In the real world the qualities discussed here are not always present. The ideal friendship is difficult for mere human beings to manage. Generally however, individuals are cognizant of these ideal qualities and use the presence or absence as a factor in characterizing their friends and friendships and in influencing their emergence.

Human Qualities of Value to Friendship

The characteristics of a friend are determining factors of the kind of relating possible, the strength, and the meaning of the relationship. Cicero claimed "Virtue [is] the one thing indispensable to friendship...." (Cicero, p. 80, 1967). For Aristotle also, virtue was essential. Virtue can be a quality one possesses or as something to strive toward. It could also be viewed as a mood, a nurturant atmosphere for friendship development.

According to Cicero, friendship is possible even for one who has not reached the pinnacle of the ideal; is not yet a virtuous man. In this way "virtue both engenders and subsumes friendship." Virtue cannot only create an milieu for friendship, but it is also essential for continuing friendship. Since virtue is unchangeable (an ideal) it stabilizes friendship. "It is Virtue...that both solidifies and preserves friendships. For in Virtue there is a harmony of affairs, a stability, a constancy...." (Cicero, p.79, 1967).

Friendship does well with a number of other qualities all of which grow as the friendship grows. Openness is one such quality which allows friends to get to know each other. Knowing the needs, desires, and concerns of the other makes for more comfortable relating. Without this knowledge there is much room for questioning, suspicion and fear. Such negative feelings cannot lead to the development of a

healthy atmosphere for close relating. There must also be a degree of faith in all dealings with others. This faith assumes the good in humankind and allows one to be open and to risk making overtures toward relation.

After extensive study Sidney Jourard and others have concluded that self-disclosure produces a number of positive consequences. According to Jourard mutual self-disclosure "is what differentiates personal relationships of love and friendship from formal role relations [because] the participants seek to make their subjective worlds known to one another, in an ongoing dialogue." Self-disclosure has also been found to be significant as a way of developing a strong relationship and in promoting psychological health and growth (Jourard, p. 222, 1974).

Associated with self-disclosure is the notion of being real, congruent, or honest about presentation of self. Lepp says "What is important for sincerity in friendship is that we reveal ourselves to our friend as we are, without pretense or mask, without affectation or deception" (p. 56, 1966). Congruence is considered therapeutic and is part of the requirements of a good therapeutic relationship according to Carl Rogers. Within the therapeutic relationship congruence permits greater knowledge and increased ability to accept, like, and help the client (Rogers, p. 51, 64, 157, 1961). Congruence has, of course, similar values in friendship.

Truthfulness is another element in the composite of values in friendship. A common quote of Emerson's describes it well. "A friend," says Emerson, "is a person with whom I may be sincere. Before him, I may think aloud...and may deal with him with...Simplicity and wholeness" (p. 98, 1969). One can be truthful about oneself with another and it is only because of this truthfulness that the other is not fearful of being truthful in return.

In order to be trusted, one must prove worthy of this trust. A trustworthy person is reliable. An honest person's actions prove trustworthiness. The action is circular for the friendship needs and provides an atmosphere of honesty and trust through the values of virtue, openness, congruence, and these values then support the atmosphere of honesty and trust.

Closely akin to trust, researchers Argyle and Henderson, found that keeping confidences was important to friends. In their research exploring rules of friendship, they also found that respecting privacy was a valued behavior by a friend (Argyle and Henderson, p. 214, 232, 1984).

The element of commitment is a salient part of a relationship.

Although sometimes considered a "casual relationship" without the necessity of any reassurance, friendship needs commitment. If, as has been so far displayed, friendship requires real honesty, openness, risking, if it demands virtue, work, energy, tolerance and patience, surely that constitutes an enormous investment by a friend. Some desire for assurance that this investment is not wasted is only natural. A friend wants reassurance of the other's concern and therefore seeks commitment.

The sociologist Georg Simmel believes people are committed to each other through obligations developed during the formation of a relationship. Simmel's concept of gratitude assures commitment. For Simmel, gratitude works in areas where legal assurance is not appropriate as with a personal relationship. (Legality, for example, is available for protection in a business investment where the courts may be used to make restitution for losses.) One becomes ingratiated through received benefits. One can never fully repay these benefits since it is not purely what is given but the act of giving which has the greatest significance. Thus gratitude toward another guarantees continued association because of the existing debt (Simmel, p. 382, 389, 1964).

Friendship also needs understanding and sensitivity. It is necessary to be able to recognize a friend's feelings, difficulties, discomforts and be empathetic and willing to offer assistance.

It is obvious, with the above list of personal values useful in friendship, that it is a demanding relationship. It does not simply happen and it will not continue without some serious involvement and labor. Friendship needs patience for it would never get past initial acquaintance if one were not willing to sow the seeds, cultivate them and make adjustments for conditions.

Conditions for the Development and Continuation of Friendship

Even with two persons who have inordinate amounts of the valuable personal qualities and the presence of the pre-requisite conditions that set the stage for relating, friendship may not flourish unless carefully nurtured with a variety of supporting and stimulating conditions. Once people get to know one another and have the desire to become good friends, there is work involved. The relationship needs constant and continual care.

Of the several exigent conditions to maintain an atmosphere for friendship, communication appears the most obvious. The need for understanding and knowledge of the other necessitates communication. However, communication is not limited to face-to-face verbal discussion between friends. There are, in friendship, as with all types of relating, non-verbal aspects of communication which are significant in providing information.

People do not have to be face-to-face to communicate. Letters, phone calls, and communication through third parties are other possible methods of sending messages. Today letters are less common and they, like the other methods, because of the lack of presence of the other, are not as valuable a medium for communication as face-to-face interaction which allows the important component of non-verbal communication to be used. Body language, gestures, eye contact, and intonations are important. In fact, communication experts consider non-verbal communication makes up far more of the emotional exchange than the verbal component. Interactive communication involves sending a message and receiving a response. If an individual sends a message and does not know the reaction to or questions raised by the message he or she cannot deal in a reasonable way with the message he or she is sending. So the communication pattern itself is critical.

Absence of communication can cause a problem. Lack of words does not itself constitute lack of communication just as communication is not always present with verbiage. Silence in direct face-to-face encounters is hard to sustain and may be a type of communication. The silence that can ensue from lack of opportunity for personal contact can be problematic to a relationship. If friends do not inevitably cross each other's paths periodically then silence will be the mode unless specific remedies are taken. Someone must initiate contact. A friend who moves away cannot remain a friend unless special means for communication are undertaken.

Silence can be a plague. It can eat away at a relationship because no one can read clearly the message it gives. Lack of communication may indicate disinterest in the continuation of the relationship. Projections, confusion, and discomfort may result. Communication is necessary for the friendship to continue as both a means to understanding the relationship and in making obvious a desire to continue the relationship. But communication requires energy. It does not happen on its own.

Acceptance is also crucial to real friendship. Friends accept both the person and the underlying values though occasional behaviors

of a friend may not be wholly accepted. Acceptance is also an essential therapeutic quality permitting the client to feel cared for and free from demanding expectations. It allows the client to explore and discuss troublesome personal issues that have created a need or desire for therapy in the first place (Rogers, 1961). Acceptance is another quality held in common by friendship and therapy.

The interaction in friendship is complex indeed. Part of this complexity is the interdependent functioning so conducive to development and sustenance of friendship. An interdependent relationship involves persons who are neither solipsistically independent nor submissively dependent. Rather it is a careful mixture of compromise and non-conformity. It is epitomized by collaboration rather than competition; equality rather than a position of supremacy on the one hand or an attitude of laissez faire on the other.

Interdependence includes elements of relation, which permits support and caring; and freedom, which permits individuality and solitude. Both these constituents of interdependence are features necessary for a well-functioning relationship and for two separate well-functioning individuals.

There has been a good deal of research recently that supports the notion that periods of solitude, aloneness, privacy, even seclusion are valuable for development of a healthy personality; one which is able to return from private rustication to fuller, more trouble free relating with others. We all need some time to ourselves but there is also a potential problem in making a separation from others for as Buber explains, we may opt for the ofttimes easier position of isolation and hestitate to return to relation (Buber, 1970).

Friendship is a relationship which will not permit possessiveness. It must allow two separate persons to work in cooperation without one overcoming the other. Freedom is an important criteria in friendship.

It is a tension between unity and separateness that is interdependence and it is this state that is optimal for both individuals to function as individuals and still be friends. Interdependence is not an easy thing to accomplish. It requires energy and work, as well as an interwoven concern for oneself and for one's friend.

A number of philosophers have considered how people actually maintain the proper tension, the careful mixture of being close yet distinct. According to MacMurray and DePaoli, people are constituted by their relations with others. Since it is a fact that "a person exists and functions only with the help of other persons, he has the power to

decide *how* he will be united with others, but not *whether* he will be united with them" (DePaoli, p. 209, 1971). DePaoli explains that one's mutuality or interconnectedness with others is fully realized when one's freedom is also completely obtained. It is only through mutual interdependence that real freedom can be found. Thus the fullness of life is found in the paradox between giving one's self to the other and being free and independent at the very same time.

Philosophical discussion of this issue of separateness and unity has been going on for centuries. It was Aristophanes who noted that man is really an unnatural half of the full hermaphrodite (a complete being with four arms, legs and so forth). It is because of the awareness of incompleteness that people seek complete physical unity and, says Aristophanes, long to unite souls as well (Plato, p. 59-65, 1951). Montaigne's discourse on friendship agrees with the notion put forth by Aristophanes. In friendship the two "mingle and merge together with so complete a blending that they efface and can no longer find the seam that joined them" (Montaigne, p. 65, 1949).

Friendship is not union where the two are subsumed and thus lost, within the relationship that people seek. According to Aristotle it is one soul with two bodies. Similarly Lepp talks of a communion of spirit. The "spiritual communion" with a friend is a communication not of the purely verbal order but a communication

> ...with the intimate life of another [which] necessarily transcends the domain of having those exchanges of the objective order which are essential to fellowship and even erotic love. It is the direct exchange of one being with another, that is to say veritable communion which friendship demands and encourages. Friendship is by nature a spiritual communion (Lepp, p. 111-2, 1966).

Friendship is structured as intersubjectivity or communion. According to Sadler an *I and Thou* create a *We*, a duality of existence, but not a union (Sadler, p. 183, 1970).

In all types of relations people have a responsibility to the others because their actions affect others' lives. A friend has more influence on his or her friend than in relations of less significance. For example a friend's moving, or working on weekends, affects the relationship. This is not to suggest that one should or can alter decisions solely on the basis of a friend's needs or wants. But it is

important to recognize the effect and influence one can have on others so that one can act in a responsible fashion.

The responsible person is a rational person. As a voluntary association, friendship involves choice and this should involve reason. It is not necessary to be aware of all the alternatives or have the action of reasoning always at the forefront of consciousness to effect reasoned behavior. If such were the case it would be difficult to form a notion of reason in many things that people do.

Reason is especially clear in the beginning of a friendship. People choose constantly in situations where they are introduced or meet by chance. They work at continuing the conversation or move out of the situation. As the beginning stages continue, habit is not yet involved and a special effort must be put forth if friendship is going to develop. Friendship eventually becomes partly habituated but since friendship is also a drain on energy, this habit can be discontinued. Without the presence of rationality, friendship becomes a haphazard association, a matter of convenience, and a true intensive relationship may fade.

An intentionality, or readiness for relation, also is present. Because friends' lives don't intersect automatically they must think about their continued relationship in order to maintain it. It requires intentional meetings, communication, and work. There is no social mandate that will encourage friendship, therefore it is left solely to the participants. Friendship develops over time and it depends on rationality and intentionality in order to continue beyond the beginning stages.

Phenomenological Aspects

Exploring the felt experience of being a friend is a somewhat different perspective than that used in discussing the conditions salient for friendship above. It would be possible to consider several of those conditions from a phenomenological perspective yet as described above they are able to stand alone as "oughts" whereas the aspects discussed as phenomenological are of a different sort in the lived world of friendship.

Friendship as a personal relation could be called an intimate relationship. A good friendship is not necessarily experienced as intimate at all times and the composition of interaction need not always appear significant. But the relationship allows the two friends to feel they know each other well and care for each other. They feel

emotionally close; a part of each other's lives. The two experience the intensity, the connectedness and significance of their relationship. An intimate relationship has a depth which social relations do not have. Intimacy is found "between partners rather than within each individual" (Acitelli and Duck, p. 298, 1987). As intimacy is not something each brings but which develops from the relationship, its impact is great. There is intensity such that more seems to be compacted in a smaller amount of time. The intimate friendship suggests a long-term commitment. It is not a capricious or expedient association. The intensity and duration tend to allow for investment through self-disclosure and increasing knowledge of each other. Intimate friends understand each other because of caring, empathy, and a good deal of experience with each other.

Love is a part of the intimate friendship. The disinclination to label friendship a love relationship is due to a fear of misinterpretation and to an enormous variation in the usage of the word love. Love can be translated as enjoyment, appreciation, sex, deep caring with a host of other variations. We use the term love in reference to inanimate objects, experiences, and all kinds of relationships thus confusion results.

The Greeks were more definitive when discussing love. Although it is unlikely that Greeks used the term love when they discussed how much they enjoyed their lamb with mint jelly or how much they liked going to a recent play at the theatre, they did discuss love of persons and designated different categories of love dependent on the feelings involved in the relation. Although there is still some confusion even with the Greek categories: eros, agape, and philia, these subdivisions allow a somewhat more distinctive characterization of the love in friendship.

The Greek typology if helpful. Eros is often perceived to be synonymous with sexual desire. The translation of the Greek term is more precisely understood as affection kindled by physical beauty or passion stimulated through attraction. According to this definition eros is selfish and ego-centered with a desire for self ascendence. Eros is a possessive love, dependent on the quality of its object, it is therefore not spontaneous but causal (Sorokin, p. 4-5, 1950). According to Tillich, eros is the desire for self-fulfillment by the other (p. 114-115, 1957). D'Arcy notes that "eros should stand for both the ecstatic, irrational and self-effacing mood of love, and the rational, self-assertive and possessive form..." of love (p. 33, 1947). Thus with D'Arcy's description there is the notion of excited energy toward the loved one,

not simply a calculated attempt at self-satisfaction.

Agape is universal, unconditional, unalterable love for the other. It is entirely unselfish and freely given. It is completely separate from reciprocity or any need for return (Outka, p. 18, 1972). Both agape and eros are one way relations (Burnaby, p. 19, 1983). Eros needs fulfillment, a coming into self; agape is a flowing out of love.

Philia is a mutual relationship between people "served and expressed by cooperation for satisfying the other's needs...." (Burnaby, p. 19, 1938). It is a "mutual relation, a bond which links two centers of consciousness in one (D'Arcy, p. 108, 1947). A strict translation of philia is friendship, a solidarity among humans (Pieper, p. 13, 1974).

Lepp notes that love and friendship are not the same because love is emotionally grounded and friendship is rationally grounded on the spiritual which is more permanent than emotional love (Lepp, p. 49-51, 1966). But Buber perhaps explains it more appropriately without distinguishing the labels used for relations and only considering the felt experience within his I-Thou relationship. To him love is more than an emotion.

> Love is the responsibility of an I for a [Thou]....
> Feelings accompany the metaphysical and metapsychical fact of love, but they do not constitute it....Feelings one "has"; love occurs. Feelings dwell in man, but man dwells in his love (Buber, p. 66, 1970).

Love involves feelings but it is not synonymous with feelings. The responsibility Buber speaks of is based on the love going out to another. It is an active concern for the other, an intentional, responsible love, that makes friendship essentially altruistic. One is motivated by generosity, not by subsequent reward. Maslow suggests that a higher state of actualization allows a more altrusitic approach where D-love (deficiency need for love) is replaced by B-love (being love) which is less needful and dependent and more autonomous and giving (Maslow, 1968).

Love is inherent in friendship. As individuals are not stagnant but vital and constantly changing, so are their moods of love toward others. Love in friendship may be an intermingling of eros, agape, and philia. Agape is a pre-condition to the development of friendship which allows one to go out to the other. Friendship (that of the personal relational type described here) can be found without eros but not

without philia. Love in friendship cannot be self-contained but must go out to the other.

Love is subjective, not objective in nature. As Buber points out an objective attitude distances one from the other or makes real relationship impossible. The uniqueness and subjective quality of the other is the focus of the love. As an object, a friend loses unique personhood and the relation can be no more than one of utility.

Friends who love each other as subjects experience a communion or "mutual indwelling" as Thomas Acquinas describes it. Sadler states that the intersubjectivity of love "transports the individual outside himself toward the other person" (p. 191, 1969). Or as Buber says the "love does not cling to an I, as if the You were merely its 'content' or object; it is between I and You" (p. 66, 1970).

Buber finds the place of meeting of two people in "the between." "Spirit is not the I but between I and You" (p. 89, 1970). The intersubjective world is a common world of We, built together, according to Buber.

This world of We must be experienced as equals: "...friendship is said to be equality..." (Aristotle, p. 224, 1962).   An unequal relationship creates a friendship of utility but not a friendship of virtue. Inequality sets up a situation where one gives more than the other and feelings of incompetence or resentment may develop.

Society censors and inhibits association where there is great disparity in monetary holdings, in age, and especially in situations of age and sex disparities combined, because exploitation is likely. In Suttles' article "Friendship as a Social Institution" the problem of inequality in friendship is discussed.

> Across status barriers, invitations to friendship arouse suspicions because they may denote either a conflict of interest or ulterior motives.... The very fact of status differences, then, undermines the basis of friendship, which is the assumption that individuals are acting of their own will rather than out of calculation or connivance (Suttles, p. 120, 1970).

How is it possible to balance the scale with two unique persons of unequal abilities, knowledge and other diverse qualities. People are multi-dimensional and cannot be easily equated. A number of theorists have attempted to deal with equality among people.

Aristotle struggled to adjust for slight inequality through the

concept of proportionality. Proportionality assumed more is required of the lesser to make up for the worthiness of the greater. This sets a workable means of exchange. Aristotle's writing on friendship seems to indicate exchange only on a material plane (although his concerns range far beyond the material) and such interaction may be easily monitored by equalizing through proportionality. But material aspects of friendship are only one way of interacting and may in fact, be the least important. Therefore, equality cannot be successfully obtained by securing symmetry (Aristotle, 1962).

According to Simmel, "sociation" itself requires the persons to act as if they were equal. An "artificial world" is promoted where persons arrange their roles to make the circumstances appropriate for interaction (Simmel, p. 48-9, 1964). It would be appropriate for people to assume various behaviors, representative of themselves, in order to meet the existential situation thus acting "as if."

MacMurray draws a more accurate definition of equality appropriate to persons rather than roles. He holds that persons relate as equals.

> This does not mean that they have, as a matter of fact, equal abilities, equal rights, equal functions or any other kind of *de facto* equality. The equality is intentional: it is an aspect of mutuality of the relation. If it were not an equal relation, the motivation would be negative; a relation in which one was using the other as a means to his own end (MacMurray, p. 158, 1961).

In other words, MacMurray sees the structure of equality emerging from a desire of persons to be equal, for the enhancement of association between persons. An intentional attitude alone does not produce equality, yet if both persons see themselves as equal, act as equals, without negating differences, equality develops.

This equality is of a spiritual sort. A friend does not judge or critique the other. There is no intentional distancing by either placing the other in an inferior or superior position, which would distance the individuals and disrupt communication and relation.

Relations such as doctor-patient, wife-husband, teacher-student, parent-child have assumed titles signifying disparity. Therefore inequality is created from the start. A friendship is seen as friend-friend, where equality is present in the beginning. In addition, equality

flourishes as friends share experiences and develop an area of mutual life. (Note Millet, 1951.)

Conclusion

We have seen that there are a number of components to friendship. It involves the presence of another, both physically and psychologically, in order to initiate relationship. The initiation is, as with the sustaining of friendship, an intentional, rational undertaking and requires communication. Although friendship is definitely distinctive from individual functioning it does not permit absorption but connected, interdependent functioning. Values of virtue, openness, truthfulness, faith, and commitment are necessary for a strong friendship to survive. The felt experience of friendship includes intensity, love, subjectivity, and equality. Although friendship is often observed to be simplistic, without form or core, the experience of intimate friendship is far more deep and compelling. Friends are immersed within the entity of friendship and understand its working more completely than can the observer.

One other phenomenological aspect, that of reciprocity, is essential to friendship. Because of the complexity of reciprocity it will be necessary to consider it at some length. The next two chapters will explore reciprocity as it exists in various relations, and an additional chapter will discuss reciprocity specific to friendship itself.

Chapter 5

Reciprocity: The Dynamics of Interaction

Reciprocity is essential for all human interaction. It is the axial component around which all relating revolves. The philosopher Martin Buber, whose writings focused on relation with others, succinctly stated the prominence of reciprocity to relation by equating the two. "Relation is reciprocity," according to Buber (p. 67, 1970). Buber is not alone in his assertion that reciprocity is the very core of relating. A number of theorists consider it fundamental to relation.

The term reciprocity appears in writings in the field of sociology, psychology, anthropology, philosophy, and law and although the concept of reciprocity has some similarities in these different disciplines there are differing shades and degrees of meaning. The meaning is assumed to be implicit and there is little explanation given. With a few exceptions the term reciprocity is used in the study of human relations without definition. Still the concept of reciprocity implies a broader intention than other comparable terms.

Broadly speaking reciprocity is the principle of give and take, yet the full meaning of the term cannot be conveyed by this simple definition. Reciprocity is a complex concept with variations in differing contexts. Since the term is used in many disciplines, as the correlation between persons, elucidation of the meaning of the term will best be accomplished by using an interdisciplinary perspective.

Overview of Reciprocity

A brief overview of the use of the term reciprocity in various disciplines will provide a foundation with which to build a more comprehensive understanding. Because of the breadth of usage of the term reciprocity other theorists have themselves employed an interdisciplinary perspective.

As a rule anthropologists have used the term to refer to exchanges between peoples in the cultures they have observed. A number of anthropologists have used the term, undefined, while others have had their explanations of exchange labelled reciprocity by other writers.

Sociologists generally consider the social exchange theory of George Homans to be a definition of reciprocity. (See further

discussion of social exchange theories below.) Several sociologists have used Homans' theory as a stepping off point for further elaboration or critiqued this theory as a means of improving understanding of reciprocity. Alvin Gouldner is a rare sociologist in setting out specifically to develop an understanding of the meaning of reciprocity.

There are several sociologists who use the term in reference to dyadic interchange or small group functioning. Those sociologists come the closest to a psychological usage of the term. The significance of reciprocity in relations and group functioning is pointed out by these sociologists and psychologists but again the term is not defined.

Philosophers, as might be expected, generally visualize the quality and value of reciprocity. Philosophers who have used the term, though few in number, have tended to mean something definite and have thus defined it. Williams and deVries have each devoted an entire volume to the clarification of reciprocity.

In law, the term reciprocity is defined in *Black's Law Dictionary* as mutuality. Mutuality is then defined as "reciprocation; interchange; an acting by each of two parties; an acting in return" (*Black's Law Dictionary*, p. 1142, 1979).

This definition does little in the way of clarification. In fact, the way the terms mutuality and reciprocity are used in various writings they appear to be somewhat different in meaning rather than the same, particularly in the social sciences and philosophy. Reciprocity appears to be a broader, more encompassing interaction; mutuality is more confined and strict and generalizable in interpretation.

Reciprocal behavior is found in practice as well as a theoretical construct. It is found everywhere in the multifarious aspects of everyday life. Reciprocity is the glue that holds society together. It is responsible for social cohesion, in other words, reciprocity is responsible for the existence of society. Reciprocal interaction can be found in large divisions of society or with the very smallest segments of society. In order for reciprocity to be possible there needs to be two factions. Reciprocity can exist between two individuals or two groups of people be they small as a family unit or as large as two nations.

The existence of society is dependent on the reciprocity in two person relations and on reciprocity in larger segments of the population. The absence of reciprocity is problematic. As MacBeath notes failure of individuals to comply with reciprocity is bad for the individuals themselves and society as a whole (MacBeath, p. 132, 1952).

Both economic and social elements are built on a reciprocal framework. Mauss has studied numerous cultures. He viewed the economic and social structures and has found the economic structure is

not a natural state which allows people to fit into it and thus associate but rather exchange precedes the formation of institutions of exchange. People act reciprocally and this permits the development of a social structure (Mauss, p. 2, 1967). The practice of reciprocity precedes the formation of a structure which facilitates reciprocity. But reciprocity is also responsible for continuation of society as we know it. "Reciprocity is the structure in a dynamic sense of the responsible society....*it creates even more inter-related actions between men*, it realizes an organic complementarity of persons and groups and institutions" (Van Peursen, p. 36, 1968).

Although economic gain and utility are to a large extent the reason for formation of societies they are not always the sole reason for exchange. The relations and contracts which ensue from the exchange are certainly as important as the utilitarian aspects in many instances (Mauss, p. 70, 1967). That is, exchange (economic or otherwise) is important to the development of sociability.

Simmel notes that giving and receiving things is used as a reason for interaction. All external and internal motives that bind individuals together may be examined in respect to their implementation of the exchange which not only holds society together once it is formed but, in a large measure forms it   (Simmel, p. 388-89, 1950).

It is this reciprocal action that makes for association as personal relation or as societal interaction. Aristotle noted, "if there is exchange there is community" (Aristotle, p. 127, 1962).   By exchanging things people create common ground which in turn permits easier association.

Social Exchange Theories

Social exchange theories find their roots in the behavioral exchange theory of Homans (1961) and the reward/cost theory of Thibaut and Kelley (1959). Both of these concepts of social exchange have a decidedly behavioristic orientation.. The continuation of a Skinnerian tone in studying exchange continues at least in part because of the ease of application. A measurement of how things equate is common in social exchange research.

But it is difficult to determine whether the complexities of vibrant relationships can be captured by such equations. In their review of the literature, Hatfield, Traupman, Sprecher, Utne, and May (1985) indicate there is still much disagreement about whether an exchange

theory approach can explain the interaction that occurs in personal relationships.

Exchange and equity theories, as they are often called, are proposed by a number of researchers and theoreticians (e.g. Walster, Walster, and Berscheid, 1978; Traupmann, Petersen, Utne, and Hatfield, 1981; Holt, 1982; Lloyd, Cate, and Henton, 1982; Murstein, Cerreto, and MacDonald, 1977).

The spectrum these researchers investigate is quite broad including great expanses of relationship types, familarity, intimacy, need, etc. One fundamental problem of this research on exchange or equity is that not all intimate relationships are equivalent but measurement is based on that premise. Certainly the variations in relationship types further complicates research. In addition, perceptions and expectations vary greatly from individual to individual and dyad to dyad. This interpretation of equity of a relationship by the two people involved and/or by an outside observer is dependent on a number of uncontrolled variables.

Some of the empirical research has focused on specific types of relationships (Clark, 1985; Hatfield, et al., 1985; Holt, 1982). Notably Clark and Mills (1979) and later Clark (1985) differentiate between "exchange and communal relationships." Although this is an important distinction, the nuances within "communal relationships" are not addressed. Clearly there is an enormous spectrum of such relationships. Relationship variations of contextual and person-specific attributes seem to be missing from the studies.

Pryor and Graburn (1980) discuss exchange in an article entitled The Myth of Reciprocity. They attempt to debunk reciprocity, somewhat disdainfully labelling reciprocity an anthropological concept. It is the "ethnographic impressions rather than any type of quantiative [measures]" that Pryor and Graburn discount (p. 215). It is precisely these things that seem to this author to beg for attention. Pryor and Graburn conclude that anthropologic assumptions of "balanced exchange" depend on invisibles and thus reciprocity is a myth (p. 236-7). The research brazenly notes that their subjects' sense of reciprocity is not substantiated by their empirical data.

It is exactly this objectification of reality that this present study of reciprocity hopes to reach beyond. The concept of reciprocity, rather than that of exchange, is less encrusted and more distant from behavioristic measurement. A phenomenological view of reciprocity, that which is experienced, not just observed, is the exploration here.

Conditions for Reciprocity

Reciprocity is give and take, an interchange between two factions. This give and take can be a very simplistic happening and involve exchange of one thing for its material equivalent, exchange of tit for tat, or it can be of a less materialistic nature where equity is difficult to measure.

The formal, and often the social, relation tend to require quid pro quo exchange. In personal relations the kinds of exchanges that are made with material items, personal involvement, energy, and time are usually not weighted and calculated.

Although reciprocity is a common phenomenon, it is not automatic. Reciprocity requires certain fundamental conditions. Some sociological theorists depict the sufficient conditions for reciprocity as mere presence of two people together. Relating involves more than presence. Although people present on a street corner may be together in reference to space, such a collection does not constitute any relation and does not imply any reciprocity. There must be awareness of the presence of the other for reciprocity to occur. Both people must recognize the other, acknowledge the other's presence and be fully present to the other.

Equality

Equality is facilitative of reciprocal interaction. Inequality which exists as status, wealth, education or cultural differences tends to work against interaction. If there exists great differences between persons the relationship which develops is likely to be lopsided. Although lopsided relations exist they are generally short lived or explicitly purposeful. Calculation, utilitarianism, and exploitation become the reason for the interaction between unequals and one person loses in the relation. This is the competitive model of association. Equality, on the other hand, allows for "collateral" influence and thus permits reciprocity and cooperation (Piaget, p. 107, 1965).

There are two main types of equality, concrete and created equality. A concrete equality exists where individuals are equal in status, wealth, and abilities. This makes development of relations much simpler and enhances interaction. It is, however, a rare occurrence. Created equality credits each with equal status because status differences are unimportant to the purpose of the relation.

Equality can be created in personal or non-personal relations. Non-personal relations may have temporarily created equality. A reciprocal exchange of materials such as groceries for money does not need to take into account anything but the items of exchange. The reciprocal act occurs for a specific purpose only and the importance of the exchange is found within the objects therefore the equality merely needs to exist between the objects-possessed-by-persons. Thus persons can act reciprocally when not in a relation which needs a larger sustaining basis of equality.

In personal relationships created equality is developed by mutual agreement but needs to last beyond the short time span of the single exchange. The equality then, must be more broadly based and accepted by both persons in the relationship. The relationship is one of equivalence because the two take it to be equivalent. As Gould explains it,

> the agents [freely acting humans] themselves define the equivalence of their reciprocal actions. Thus the equivalence is not to be understood as pre-existing or pre-given, but is rather constituted by their understanding and free agreement....It should be added that the equivalence which the agents determine need not be taken in narrow sense to refer to an equivalence between single actions, but may refer to sets of actions (Gould, p. 7-8, 38, 1977).

In other words, the status differences which might exist in the external world are unimportant to the relationship. This assumed or created equality continues to exist during the duration of the relationship.

Equality must exist in the motion of reciprocity itself. That is to say, there must be a degree of equality in the actual giving and receiving. (Equality is not understood here to mean sameness in giving and receiving which would not be very useful in most cases.) If one continually gives, giving may become a means of control whereby the other is constantly indebted. If one continually receives without giving, receiving may become an act of exploitation.

Ultimately, giving and receiving depend on needs, abilities, and resources but the kind and nature of the giving and receiving can be altered to meet the circumstances and still be equitable to both sides. People do not have to be the same in order to relate. The resources of different business people are different, as are their abilities, but the

interaction must contain a sense of equivalency if both are to fare reasonably in their association.

The Dynamics of Reciprocity

A reciprocal exchange can be seen as a static occurrence but reciprocity in a relation is more appropriately viewed as a dynamic interactional process. In a personal relationship the reciprocity is continuous, not curtailed to a single exchange of items. Even the business relation is generally ongoing where two people do business in the present and expect to continue doing business with each other in the future. The association rarely stops after one exchange unless one or the other has felt the exchange was unequal (in this case the benefit was not equal to the cost) or the relation was not truly reciprocal. In a personal relationship because the relationship signifies continuation of giving and receiving the expectation of future exchange dissuades any weighing of equality. It is assumed that things will equal out over time.

In addition to seeing reciprocity as an ongoing interchange between people it is dynamic in another sense. Reciprocity doesn't just *happen*. It requires active participants. Giving is not a passive act, neither is receiving. If the other simply accepts in a passive way rather than active receiving, there is not really exchange going on. Without active receiving something is not given to another but only given away. The absence of active giving assumes that something is taken, i.e. stolen.

The dynamic of reciprocity is interaction. The involvement of physical, mental, and emotional presence makes reciprocity more complete and interaction can be immediate and direct. Reciprocity is not a linear, one way event. Reciprocity is not the same as response. Instead of static givers and receivers there is a coexistent action of giving and receiving, the two are active at the same time, one in the converse position of the other.

Wilmot gives a good example of reciprocity in his discussion of the transactional nature of communication. He notes that transactional dyadic communication is not action-reaction. Instead of "senders" and "receivers" in communication there is simultaneous sending and receiving by each participant. One speaks and observes the reception of that speech by the other. Non-verbal communication is also a significant part of what is communicated. All aspects are inter-related so that one person influences the other and vice versa, and one

element of communication pattern and content influence other elements. There is a constant feedback that influences the developing communication (Wilmot, p. 8-10, 1975).

Reciprocity's giving and receiving is like an action-counter-action where the action is contingent on the expected counter-action and the counter-action takes into consideration the action that has occurred. Reciprocity incorporates give-and-take so that the manner of the giving is dependent on the manner of the taking and subsequent giving. Giving and receiving are intertwined, correspondingly dependent acts.

Gould explains that the interaction of reciprocity is not a cause and effect situation. Within a relation, reciprocity is different than one time exchanges made between people who remain strangers. Within a relation causality explains connection between subject and object, but it cannot explain connections of subject and subject because subjects, or agents, are not reactive. They have freedom of choice and intentional action. Gould describes a reciprocal social relation as one in which

> each agent acts with respect to the other on the basis
> of a shared understanding, and a free agreement, to the
> effect that the actions of one with respect to the other
> are equivalent to the actions of the other with respect
> to the first (Gould, p. 38, 1977).

The interaction between the two is not causal one to the other but each does take the other into consideration.

Parsons and Shils elaborate the inter-related structure of the true interaction of two people. The action of the one person is oriented by his interpretations of the other's action and is also based on his expectation of the other's reaction to his behavior (Parsons and Shils, p. 87, 1969). A person does not simply react but digests what the other has portrayed and anticipates how the other will interpret his future behavior.

Schutz describes interaction in a similar fashion. The situation of face-to-face encounter involves anticipation of the other's behavior. One plans one's own action according to projections in fantasy of the other's expected behavior based on past experience with the other. One's action is governed by one's understanding of the social world and consideration of the expected action which one's behavior will promote in the other (Schutz, p. 141, 194, 181, 1970).

The interaction is the intermingling of the two persons' behavior, influence, interpretations, and expectations. Reciprocity is circular interaction. The cycle, however, must have a beginning.

Mauss explains how the cycle is initiated. In cultures observed by Mauss a gift is given by one person who seeks an association with another person. It is only when there is a return gift that a cycle has actually been brought into being (Mauss, p. 26, 1967). The completed reciprocal exchange constitutes a cycle and signifies that both parties have willingly joined in a relation. The cycle once begun has no ragged edges of beginnings and endings. The cycle continues now with active giving and receiving.

Reciprocity is not parallel action but interaction. Psychologists have found that childhood development includes a period of parallel play, when children play side-by-side but do not play *with* each other. This is not interaction but simultaneous individual action. This type of action is not curtailed to childhood. It can be found frequently in adult conversation and behavior. Although not always obvious, egocentric behavior is non-interactive. Such simultaneous individual action is not real reciprocity.

Gouldner points out an instance of parallel action in his distinction between reciprocity and complementarity, which he criticizes others for not recognizing. Gouldner assesses complementarity to mean that "one's rights are another's obligations" (p. 167, 1960). In other words, in complementarity, A has rights and B has obligations. There is therefore no need for exchange, only for B to pay his due. If the dynamics of reciprocity are stopped, as when looking at one frame of a motion picture, this is indeed the situation. But reciprocity is the moving picture, a continued complementarity, not a solidified moment within a relation. Thus at a given point in time, one person may in fact have obligations and the other have rights but in the motion of reciprocity, these moments are difficult to discern.

In a personal relationship, there is a concern for *the other* present within the dealings. Altruistic behavior is substituted for egocentric behavior. Because of this concern for the other, action is more intermingled than Gouldner portrays. Gouldner states that reciprocity and complementarity are by no means identical. This is true in the sense that complemenetarity is not the same as, but only one segment of, the continuous motion of reciprocity.

Reciprocity can be seen as collaboration. Cooperation is often mere give and take but collaboration is sensitivity to the other where there is "mutual satisfaction" (Sullivan, p. 246, 1953). Collaboration is concerned with *we* not merely what must be done with the other in order to best satisfy one's own needs. Collaboration involves two persons working together at the same task. One person poses an idea,

the other builds on that idea, together they build an expanded notion better than either could have done alone.

Reciprocity could also been described as symmetry. Symmetry involves two persons in doing the same thing. Together they accomplish what neither could have done alone. To move a heavy object may require the joint action of two people. They both do the same thing, yet one alone could not accomplish the task. If two people talk on the telephone for example, both are doing the same thing but neither could do it alone.

In a relationship it is most likely that the reciprocity will involve complementarity, symmetry, and collaborative action intermingled at different times.

The Content and Process of Reciprocity

The dynamics of reciprocity have been explored. Reciprocity is action, an interaction. A main point of confusion with reciprocity is the mixing of the *what* of reciprocity with the *why* of reciprocity. Reciprocity is the exchange of many different types of things. These things constitute the what. Often reciprocity occurs for the sole purpose of effecting an exchange of materials. There is also reciprocity which uses things for exchange but with a purpose that is beyond the actual things themselves. This purpose could be called the spirit of reciprocity. Reciprocity could also, here, be rightfully divided into the content (what) and process (why).

The Content of Exchange

The exchange of material things has a motive (or purpose) of utilitarianism. Paying money for food, clothing, lodging, transportation, and the like is exchanging something which is imbued with societal exchange value for something needed and thus of value to the purchaser. This sort of exchange goes on constantly in the market place and the business world. Money is a medium of exchange. Its purpose is to facilitate exchange. By making something of interchangeable value, such as money, one does not need to go through a number of specific exchanges in order to secure what is actually needed. It also provides a way of exchanging material for non-material things. Thus services of one may be easily exchanged for the materials of another. A utilitarian purpose may not be entirely obvious on the

surface. For example a child may give gifts at Christmas for the purpose of receiving gifts in return. Although children are generally more overt about their egocentricism, it is not at all unusual for adults to have utilitarian intentions at the root of an apparently altruistic action.

Reciprocity can involve an exchange of many types of things. Foa and Foa have developed a schema of resource exchange. A "*resource* is anything transacted in an interperesonal situation" and these resources can be "concrete or symbolic" according to Foa and Foa (p. 78, 1980). The six classes of resources outlined include: love, status, information, money, goods, and services (p. 79, 1980). They go on to describe what these resources are, how they relate to each other, and the salience of the resource provider.

Exchange involving money or exchange of professional services are probably the most clear-cut, solely for the sake of material gain. In other areas of exchange, separating the object from the process is much more difficult.

Many exchanges occur outside the market place. Neighbors exchange help with household and yard tasks. Gifts may be exchanged. Even time could be considered a "commodity" that is exchanged since that seems to be a very valuable resource in our fast-paced world. The intellectual realm may serve as a focus for exchange. People may exchange ideas and concepts and use others' ideas to build on in a synergetic manner. Advice is often exchanged when people are of equal status. One is more willing to receive advice from an associate who is also willing to receive advice in turn. There is, then, an exchange of influence.

There may be exchange on an emotional level. If, for example, a neighbor is sick, concern for this neighbor may elicit one's assuming responsibility for him or her. This may take the form of taking over the neighbor's outside responsibilities, such as shopping, in order to help meet external demands. The concern may involve nursing the neighbor back to health; the neighbor needs to make some return for this concern. This may be accomplished by helping out when the caregiver is away on vacation or the neighbor may buy a gift for the caregiver, not to pay her off but to indicate that the help was valued. A thank you is, in a manner of speaking, a repayment in appreciation, although not always sufficient repayment. The determination or repayment is based on the value the care has in the eyes of the one who has received it and the clarity of expectations of the care-giver for a return.

An assessment is often made as to the ability to repay in similar fashion. For example, an elderly neighbor may not be able to return help with yard work for that type of help given. And it may not be possible for the elderly neighbor, on a fixed income, to give a gift in response to assistance given. The elderly neighbor most likely will reciprocate in some manner, yet the response is different dependent on the players in the interaction.

The schema of resources proposed by Foa and Foa includes a contextual dimension of "particularistic versus universal." In this way, interactions in varying relation types are distinctive. So one is more universal in exchange of lawyer or doctor resources but "particularistic with regard to a friend, a spouse, or a mother" (p. 79, 1980). The who of reciprocity directly impacts on how the content of exchange is perceived.

The Process of Exchange

The *what* of exchange is, as has been noted, not usually free from its connection with the *why*. The exchange of things often has as its main purpose the development of an association. The action of reciprocity, in other words, is undertaken to effect a relation. As Buber said "relation is reciprocity" and the "purpose of relation is the relation itself - touching the You" (Buber, p. 67, 113, 1970). Things can be exchanged for the purpose of relation with no intent, in fact, no interest in the actual things exchanged, where no material gain is expected.

Dialogue is an exchange. Often the purpose of communication is the association, not the content of the talk. "The fundamental fact of human existence is man with man....language is only a sign and a means for it...." (Buber, p. 203, 1965a). Simmel suggests "sociability presents perhaps the only case in which talk is its own legitimate purpose." According to Simmel in this case, talk is "the fulfillment of a relation which wants to be nothing but relation - in which, what usually is the mere form of interaction becomes its self-sufficient content" (Simmel, p. 53, 1964).

The relation, the meeting as Buber calls it, is found in the coming together around some topic. When people talk about the weather, it is rarely because the weather needs to be discussed. Conversations at parties may have ulterior motives such as finding out specific things about another, but generally such conversations are for the purpose of meeting each other in the form of words. In discussion

where the content is of a more substantive nature than the weather, the process still may be of concern to the two persons talking.

Millet points out value in the process of exchange in the intellectual realm, specifically in friendship. The intellectual focus becomes the "medium of exchange" (Millet, p. 207, 1951). People often talk about things of interest, not to convince one another or to necessarily build a theory or even provide information but as a means to relation. This seems to be often true in collegial relations which may or may not also involve people who consider themselves friends.

A clear case of exchange for the enjoyment of association is the game. Children play together not simply to win or to create something, not for some end goal. Children are not the exclusive users of games for association. Adults play bridge, scrabble, pictionary, and monopoly for the enjoyment of being together. In fact observation of such games will sometimes elucidate just how uninterested the players are in the goal of the game.

According to Buber, the reciprocity that draws out relation is not the content of reciprocity. "Man receives, and what he receives is not a 'content' but a presence, a presence of strength" (Buber, p. 158, 1970). Buber refers here to the presence of the other where the relation may be the whole purpose of reciprocal interaction.

Reciprocity as Ideal and Fact

Reciprocity has been discussed here as a theoretical construct, a value or ideal, and as a fact, which can be observed empirically. The value of reciprocity, that is the ideal, supports the existence of reciprocal action, the fact. Gouldner has referred to reciprocity as a norm. A norm is a guide or model (an ideal) for what ought to be and also an average or typical pattern (normal observable behavior) of what generally happens. Many references to the norm of reciprocity do not make this distinction. Differentiation of the two components of reciprocity will also serve to add clarity to an understanding of reciprocity.

Reciprocity as an Ideal

The ideal of reciprocity is a value in all cultures. The ideal serves as a basis for action and a basis for expectations that a response similar to the initial action will occur. This ideal leads to praxis

between different societies as in the international scene. For example, President Anwar Sadat of Egypt took some courageous steps in initiating peace negotiations with Israel. His actions were based on an assumption that there would be a reciprocal action by Israel and thus new channels of communication would be opened to these countries and a continuing reciprocal communication might provide a direction for peace. Sadat's ideal of reciprocity was expected also to be an ideal for Israel and thus was employed to elicit like action and benefit Egypt (and Israel in the long run).

When other people are understood to hold reciprocity as a value, which according to anthropological studies is a universal phenomenon, trust is established permitting the parties to engage in relation with less hesitation and fear. Reciprocity provides grounds for confidence and is in this way an initiator of relation.

The value of reciprocity continues to be significant after the relation has commenced, that is, even when reciprocity as fact is part of the relation. Because reciprocity is seen as something one should try to uphold, it promotes the relation and acts as a stabilizing feature.

An initial overture is more risky because the danger of rejection is higher. One cannot project what the other will do before association has developed. There is only the ideal of reciprocity present to allay fears. Rejection can occur in various ways from blunt refusal to polite non-interest in association. For example, a friendly greeting, an invitation to conversation, met by a single syllable response provides little equality of exchange and is a manner of rejection.

The presence of reciprocity within the beginning of a relation acts to stabilize it. As expectations of return are met each person begins to relax into a trust which now has an historical basis. There is thus, less fear and risk involved in continuing the giving and receiving. Reciprocity has been established as a norm in the initial stages of the relation. It does not act as a guarantee to continued reciprocal relation but is an indication that continued association is likely.

Reciprocity has been found by anthropologists and sociologists to be a means of initiating association and as a means to maintaining this association, in fact, to a large extent in forming and keeping society intact (Kurth, p. 159, 1970; Williams, p. 38 & 50, 1973; Simmel, p. 389, 1950; Gouldner, p.176-7, 1970; Mauss, p. 21, 24-5, 1967; Malinowski, p. 73-76, 1969).

Once reciprocity becomes part of the relation, it can strengthen the relation. As a favor is received one feels grateful and obligated to return the favor. This mutual exchange increases the possibility of

future mutual exchange (Blau, p. 93-96, 1969). As trust is continued reciprocity is built from historical precedent.

An exchange tends to increase future exchange, for example, liking tends to produce further association which increases liking (Argyle, p. 62, 1983). This developing reciprocal emotion tends toward escalation. Because A likes B, B tends to like A. A's being liked tends to produce a greater liking of B and so forth. Similar to the law of inertia, once the action of giving is put into motion it tends to remain in motion, and it will continue unless it meets with an undue amount of friction.

Reciprocity as a Fact

As a fact, reciprocity is never complete, as an ideal, it is never fully achieved. DePaoli claims that reciprocity is, at best, an intention (p. 242, 1971). It is an ideal which works toward actualization as fact. If the ideal is upheld as important with specific intent, the practice of reciprocity follows, but intent is essential. Reciprocity doesn't arise of its own accord. Although there is a natural tendency toward reciprocity one must direct attention to the practice of it. It is indeed difficult to separate reciprocity as an ideal from reciprocity as fact, for the ideal promotes the reality. The practice of reciprocity is imperative for the realization of the worth of the ideal and a force toward maintaining it as an ideal.

Reciprocity is a universal and common occurrence but how do people actually develop an understanding of reciprocity and put it into practice in their lives? Piaget claims that reciprocity must be practiced before it becomes, for the child, an aspect of his own morality. It doesn't start as a theoretical proclamation by an adult and simply get implemented in behavior. As reciprocity is practiced the child becomes more fully aware of its value and necessity in interaction with others and thus increases his ability and desire to use it. The same is true for adults as age doesn't always bring maturity.

A person's first involvement with reciprocity occurs on the biological level according to Buber. "The prenatal life of the child is a pure natural association, a flowing toward each other, a bodily reciprocity...for the womb in which it dwells is not solely that of the human mother" (p. 76, 1970). Because the biological structure of the womb is both mother and the unborn child there is truly a physiological exchange. The fetus and mother are acting in a reciprocal fashion.

The infant receives from the mother the necessary care and attention essential for its survival. In return the child gives the mother a sense of joy and fills parental needs. This reciprocal exchange again is accomplished without consciousness. The child and the mother are in a relationship. They are "the original unit of personal existence," according to MacMurray. "The motivation of the child's behavior must be reciprocal, even if the reciprocity is, to begin with, merely implicit." The relationship, although it appears to be very one-sided in responsibility and work is one of "mutual delight." The original mother-child relationship is the basis for a personal development of acquiring skills and executing intentions (MacMurray, p. 62, 63, 65, 1961).

A child's first understandable encounter with reciprocity is found within the structure of the child's first association with people, the family. This is not the only forum for its practice however. Piaget has explained the development of reciprocity in children extensively in *The moral judgement of the child.* He argues that adult authority is not sufficient to move the child to a sense of justice and understanding of reciprocity. Theoretical proclamation by the adult "do as I say" does not allow the child to learn the value reciprocity has for dealing with people. The practice of reciprocity is necessary if true understanding and continued use is to occur. Because adults and children are unequal in status (at least in age and status of authority if not other types) the adult has authority and imposes it on the child to protect and socialize the child. When the adult insists on reciprocal actions by the child through demands for sharing, equality, and justice, the act of imposition denies the presence of reciprocity between the child and adult. Reciprocal interaction is difficult for the child inexperienced in reciprocation to manage smoothly with an adult.

Peer associations, because of the equality in status, provide a milieu where there is greater possibility for the practice of reciprocity. Piaget's study of children found that the norm of reciprocity, which is the "source of the logic of relations" developed only through cooperation with other children (Piaget, p. 107, 1965). That is, understanding and the desire to use reciprocity develops through engaging in reciprocal behavior with peers, who, because of equal status, can more easily engage in exchange.

DePaoli refers to Piaget in his development of the concept of mutuality. According to DePaoli, the young child's understanding of what is right is dependent on his "unilateral respect" for the adult and recognition of adult authority and is externalized through a sense of duty and obligation. At first cooperation is caused by adult demands for it.

Later the child begins to cooperate with others because he or she thinks it is best not because he or she is animated by mutual respect. Still later in childhood, there is the development of a relation of mutuality in an atmosphere of real cooperation. The child has moved to a stage of "mutual respect." The child's inner sense of goodness is founded on "mutual respect" and goodness is synonymous with cooperation with the other in full mutuality (DePaoli, p.228-232, 1971).

The child becomes more of an individual through self respect afforded him/her and is no longer completely dependent but becomes interdependent. It is then that the child has enough confidence that she or he can afford respect to the other. This allows the laws of mutuality to come into play. The child is then sensitive to the needs of the other. Egocentricism makes way for consideration of the other and for mutual cooperation and reciprocity. The child begins to develop, at about age ten, a sensitivity to what is important to the other and what can be done to support the other (DePaoli, p. 228-232, 1971).

Piaget argues that the development of moral consciousness is determined to a large extent by the person's ability to understand and work with reciprocity. The child's concern for the other and a sense of morality is developed through actual experience of reciprocity. Children begin by practicing reciprocity and only later understand its full meaning. The child needs equals with whom to interact in order to develop a sense of this reciprocity. Friends of one's own age are a significant addition to this development. It is also necessary that reciprocity as a value, as held by the adult for whom the child has unilateral respect, be visible to the child. The adult may act as a model for the child. Again it is the ideal and the fact that are interconnected to bring reciprocity into realization (Piaget, 323, 295, 1965).

Summary

Reciprocal behavior is indeed complex. The universal expectation for reciprocity is important for initiation of interaction. Equality can facilitate reciprocal behavior.

A significant difficulty in understanding reciprocity is its dynamic nature. The dynamism involves players, things, and time, complicating a clear focus. Who, what, and when are interactive components of reciprocity each influencing the other. Reciprocity is held as an ideal at the same time it is practiced in human interaction. Experiencing reciprocity underscores the importance of the ideal while improving the likelihood of continued practice.

Chapter 6

Reciprocity in Various Relations

Interaction between people is dependent on reciprocity. "Some dimension of reciprocity is present in all social interaction," according to Gould (p. 38, 1977). The last chapter reviewed some aspects of reciprocity and indicated the extensive breadth of reciprocal behavior. This chapter will consider the different types of reciprocal behavior.

Frames of Reciprocity

Reciprocity varies in degree and kind. This variation is dependent particularly on the social and environmental contexts and the type of relation being considered. Even within a particular type of relation such as friendship, reciprocity varies in reference to the personal characteristics of the two friends and may appear different today than yesterday.

The reciprocity found in a relationship like friendship is on-going, dynamic interaction, but reciprocity can be viewed in segments, framed by time. Four major ways to frame reciprocity can be distinguished: *simultaneous giving and receiving, a reciprocal moment, a reciprocal encounter, and a reciprocal relationship.*

Simultaneous giving and receiving is easiest to see because both people give and receive at the same time. Often the exchange is of the same or similar things, such as a handshake. A *reciprocal moment* is a segment of time in which a single "cycle" of reciprocity can be bracketed. In a foreign country for example, a visitor may purchase a souvenir at a store. The proprietor and visitor engage in reciprocal behavior. They may not actually communicate in a common language but mix two languages with gestures in order to complete a single transaction. The two are unlikely to ever come in contact again. This is a reciprocal moment; a single transaction takes place. Simultaneous giving and receiving is one type of reciprocal moment.

A *reciprocal encounter* is when two people experience an event together. It is most often a face-to-face situation. Two people eat lunch together and then return separately to their respective jobs. They engaged in reciprocal behavior throughout the lunch, exchanging niceties, passing the salt, and engaging in social chatter. The exchanges can be distinguished from other reciprocity between these

two because a beginning and ending of their time together can be distinguished. The Buberian I-Thou relationship is another type of reciprocal encounter.

A *reciprocal relationship* is ongoing relating, where reciprocity has occurred, is occurring, and will occur in the future. A reciprocal relationship can include all other frames in which reciprocity is found. In a reciprocal relationship, giving and receiving may overlap. That is, one may give and give and give yet not receive in return, or one may give and receive something distinct from that which was given. The reciprocity is not necessarily like for like. Because the relationship has a future it is assumed that things will even out over time. The reciprocity may be most difficult to observe in the reciprocal relationship because it is spread out over time and the giving and receiving elements are not always clearly visible.

Reciprocity can be potential or actual. That is exchange can be occurring presently or there may be simply the expectation that exchange will occur. It is both of these that make a relationship a reciprocal relationship.

Forms of Reciprocity

In addition to the segments outlined by time frames, several divergent forms of reciprocity can be discerned. Reciprocity varies in degree and kind. The reasons people act reciprocally include business or social purposes, among others, thus the form reciprocity takes will correspondingly deviate. The form of reciprocity also influences the type of relation and social context (present circumstances) and is influenced by these things.

The form reciprocity can take is analogous to a spectrum where the light is dispersed into various colors without distinct separations. The dispersed forms of reciprocity include reciprocity as a basic social phenomenon, reciprocity as simple exchange, reciprocity as a norm, reciprocity as a moral principle, and reciprocity as intimate exchange. Although there are not distinct separations between these forms, the context, content, and process of these forms varies.

For each form of reciprocity there are several salient aspects to explore. These aspects include the motivation underlying the reciprocity, the materials exchanged, the actual dynamic motion of the reciprocity, what the expectations and demands are, and what the reciprocity provides. Examining these aspects provides a comparison

between the different forms of reciprocity and a clearer understanding of reciprocal behavior in different types of relations.

Reciprocity as a Basic Social Phenomenon

It appears that a social attitude is basic to human creatures. We are born and nurtured in a social group. We are, particularly in childhood, but also throughout life, socialized, that is, taught to fit in with our social group. Life outside of a social framework is barely fathomable. Even history's most notable recluses were not entirely outside of society but rather on the fringes. Thoreau in his solitude had three chairs in his house, "one for solitude, two for friendship, and three for society" (p. 97, 1960).

Almost all primates exist within a social order. A psychological concept holds that association is instinctual. It certainly is a biological necessity in early life. As infants and small children, homo sapiens can not survive in isolation. They are physically incapable of taking care of themselves. This need for others is a fundamental reciprocity.

There is some strong psychological evidence that physical care is not the only requirement met through social interaction with the young. Harry Harlow's studies and the earlier studies of Spitz indicate that people need the physical and psychological warmth of others. In order to survive, according to Spitz's study, children have to have some significant interaction with others. In order to learn to be a social animal, and thus survive in the social world, infants and children have to interact with adults and others their own age, according to Harlow's work (Harlow, 1958; Spitz, 1946).

Children need at least one other person to provide for their physical and psychological needs. These needs can be reasonably met in the family, a small social network. As the human matures his or her need for others doesn't disappear or even diminish although the reasons

Forms of Reciprocity

Forms of reciprocity	General or specific	Action of reciprocity	Because of motive	In order to motive
Reciprocity as a Basic Social Phenomenon	generalizable	being with others (a potential of giving and receiving	internal	self-need
Reciprocity as Simple Exchange	generalizable	give and take	external	self-gain
Reciprocity as a Norm	generalizable - prescriptive	giving and receiving - initial giving is voluntary	external	self-interested other-interested
Reciproicty as a Moral Principle	generalizable - specific only in a formal way	giving and receiving	internal	self-interested other-interested
Reciprocity as Intimate Exchange	specific and personal	giving and receiving - in the between	internal	other-interested self-interested

Forces of compulsion	Mode of requirement	Content of exchangee	Linkage	Cause of breakdown
instinctual, biologically compulsory	expectation	presense of self	initiates socialization	distancing
economic compulsion	demand	material goods	social linkage and individual gain	unsatisfactory dealings
socially compulsory	demand	material and abstract things	social cohesion	compliance rewards less than non-compliance rewards
morally compulsory	demand	material and abstract things	social cohesion	lack of moral responsibility
voluntary	expectation	abstract and material things	personal relations, units of society	continual lack of concern - lack of response

for the need change. The formation of a larger society is, in Simmel's words, founded on

> erotic instincts, objective interests, religious impulses, and purposes of defense or attack, or play or gain, of aid or instruction, and countless others cause men to live with other men, to act for them, with them, against them, and thus to arrange their conditions reciprocally... (Simmel, p. 40, 1964).

People are drawn together because of reciprocal needs and thus form a web of interaction. The society needs the various skills of different people and needs numbers for the purposes of protection. Society is a structure which has been built through reciprocity, the exchange of available personal and material resources. The society continues to exist because of this reciprocity and for the purpose of reciprocity, that is, the value that the reciprocity provides individuals within the social network.

Philosophers hold that reciprocity is the basis of existence. Humanity as we know it is found in reciprocity, on the personal level, as well as the societal level of which Simmel speaks. "A person is constituted by his relations with other persons," according to DePaoli (p. 79, 1971). One only exists through dynamic relation with others. Without this essential relation, the person, in fact does not exist. It is the relation with others that is the fundamental mode of human existence.

Verbal communication, a specifically human type of reciprocal behavior provides a good display of the fundamental aspect of relation. One learns to speak with others not as an isolate. (In fact, feral children appear not only to have no knowledge of how to speak but have lost the ability to learn having passed a critical period of development.) The purpose of learning to speak is to facilitate association with others. "Man as a speaking being exists only in reciprocity; dialogue precedes monologue; consciousness of responsiveness precedes self-consciousness" (Van Peursen, p. 29, 1968).

One develops both a sense of self and a sense of others through an association with others. As the child or adolescent leans on and pulls away from parents she or he develops some measure of security and independence. It is vital for the child to have someone to both hold to and pull away from.

Johann states that our greatest potentials are obtainable only through others. Life is contingent on others and through this continued

contingency, one is always met by the new and unpredictable and by the compelling within the new. The relation is "one of encounter - an ever ongoing exchange whose meanings do not pre-exist but grow and develop as the exchange proceeds, and depend on the love that is brought to it" (Johann, p. 122-3, 1968). It is this relation, this reciprocity or exchange which is at the basis of existence.

Reciprocity as a basic social phenomenon is generalizable and at the same time specific and personal. This paradox is created by the involvement of both intention and actualization. There is a tendency toward reciprocity because of its physical and psychological survival value, yet this tendency toward reciprocity is not easily actualized without intentionality.

Reciprocity as the basis of existence is a readiness, an opening of one's self to the other. Buber describes it this way: "In the beginning is the relation - as a category of being, as readiness, as a form that reaches out to be filled, as a model of the soul; the *a priori* of relation; *the innate you*" (Buber, p. 78, 1970). Reciprocity as a basic social phenomenon is an attitude toward others. It is an openness and a subsequent presence to others and acceptance of others. This potential is realized through intentional action.

The reciprocity is actualized as a personal and specific reciprocity. The motivation is internal. The content of exchange in reciprocity as a basic social phenomenon is the presence of the other as person, yet of a generalized nature. One's concern for the other is personal to the extent that it is extended to *any* other without reservation as is love defined as agape.

This pattern of reciprocity once established is not completely secure. Buber's dialectic of distance and relation applies here. The reciprocity one undertakes is not acquired and permanent forever. It is moved into and away from, for it is stressful to relate as well as rewarding. People get trapped into the use of distance and find the return to relation too difficult to accomplish.

Reciprocity as a basic social phenomenon provides for continued relation, for the expansion of reciprocity and for the continued growth and development of the individual.

Reciprocity as Simple Exchange

Reciprocity as simple exchange is found most commonly in the world of business. Simple exchange is exemplified in dealings with a used car salesman or store clerk, and sometimes when dealing in

social relations. No one is necessarily excluded from simple exchange procedures although other modes of reciprocity are often more appropriate. Reciprocity as simple exchange will be explained here as basically a business-type occurrence.

The motivation of reciprocity as simple exchange is that of self-interest. Reciprocity is for something not for someone. The size of the gain is of much greater consequence than any other consideration.

Money, material objects, or services are the content of exchange. The exchange always involves something concrete, measurable. The medium of exchange is non-personal allowing for easy generalization. That is, it is of little concern who enacts the exchange as long as there is competency in producing the desired outcome.

The action of reciprocity as simple exchange is clear-cut and obvious to the parties involved in the exchange and observers as well. Often negotiations precede the exchange of the material things. This is an insurance system. Since utility is the purpose of exchange, the other is depersonalized and there is little reason for confidence or trust. If the business person expects future transactions this expectation of continued reciprocity supports a trusting atmosphere. Since the content of transaction is the significant thing, a change in transactors in the future is not problematic. The actual exchange, then, following negotiation, is structured. Each understands his or her part in the proceedings and exchange is accomplished easily. An example of this might be as follows: A woman enters a clothing store. She inquires about various prices and different labels of clothing. After some deliberation about prices and styles she makes a selection and takes it to the counter to exchange her money for the store's product. The clerk at the counter is not the one who helped her obtain an overview of the various items. This clerk checks the price marked on the item. The woman purchaser checks the price rung-up on the cash register. The clerk carefully counts the money handed to her by the customer and returns the change. The customer counts the change returned to her. An entirely different cast would have produced the same transaction. The behaviors have been played through with other people at earlier times. Everyone knows the proper script for each role.

The intent is to gain in the proceedings but it must be clear to the other that it will not be at his or her expense or the exchange will not materialize for such is the nature of self protection. Each must prove to the other that what is given is not merely in like fashion but exactly equal in value.

Immediate parity is also essential. This is due partly to the absence of trust and partly due to the short-term nature of this type of reciprocity. Often a market place transaction is a one-time occurrence, a reciprocal moment. This changes the nature of the reciprocity. Whereas generally an aspect of reciprocity is its ongoing giving or cyclical nature, reciprocity as simple exchange may only entail one complete cycle.

Because of the non-personal nature and because of the short-term structure of much of simple exchange, the usual giving and receiving may appear more like give-and-take. Lack of trust plays a part in this. Each feels that she or he is getting only what is due. There is, therefore, no compunction against taking. One's obligations are fulfilled because there is a demand that they be fulfilled; there is no choice.

Self-interest is often best met by making a fair reciprocal dealing and by keeping up one's good name thus exchange in the future is facilitated. This tends to encourage an ongoing reciprocity. There are, however, outside forces which enforce reciprocal action. In simple exchange these forces are legal. If improper or unequal actions occur, one may appeal to the system of justice, the law generally, which is outside the dyad of exchange. It acts to right imbalances. Thus reciprocity as simple exchange tends to work of its own accord but has also external enforcement to encourage proper actions and punish non-compliance.

The possibility of non-reciprocal association developing and continuing is minimal. If either individual is not satisfied with the material exchange, the association is stopped. There is no personal involvement with the other which might prevent immediate withdrawal when reciprocal exchange is missing.

The extension of the market place mentality to other milieus is frequent. Some alteration may occur from the brusque and completely de-personalized character of simple exchange in the market place when it is found within personal relationships. Immediate parity is not imperative in the personal realm. For example, if you and a colleague go out to lunch and you discover you have left your wallet in your office, your colleague willingly pays the bill and does not hound you for the money immediately upon return to the office. This is due to greater trust and an expectation that the relationship will last and debts will be paid eventually. Since the relation has a future, it is assumed that the accounts will balance in future exchanges.

Simple exchange between friends is not uncommonly a burr that aggravates a good relationship. Friends (or relatives) may attempt

to avoid simple exchange unless a clear contractual basis is established at the beginning. Thus some one writes and dates an "I owe you." If professional services are provided the receiving friend may insist on an acceptable payment to the one providing services prior to receipt of services. In this way distress due to feelings of inequity can be more easily avoided. Friends may refuse to ask for material items (or services) from friends because of lack of ability to compensate.

Reciprocity as simple exchange is based on self-interest, is de-personalized and is often a short term, reciprocal moment association.

Reciprocity as a Norm

Reciprocity is often understood as a norm. A norm is defined in two distinct ways. It may be explanatory, describing the general practice, the average, what normally is expected to occur; or as a directive, a standard, a model of what ought to be, the principle of right action, a prescription. These two meanings are not unlike reciprocity as fact or ideal discussed in the previous chapter. This section will discuss the descriptive concept, reciprocity as a norm, that of the average or normal behavior. The next section will discuss the prescriptive concept, reciprocity as a moral principle, that of a standard or model of right action. Although it is difficult to separate these two as they are intertwined, awareness of these two forms of reciprocity will aid in understanding the concept of reciprocity.

Reciprocity is normative in all value systems, according to Gouldner and others. This commonness does not imply that the norm of reciprocity is the same everywhere. It varies over a wide range. Reciprocity as a norm can be seen in many settings such as business relations, family relations, or neighbor relations. In all these instances people are expected to act reciprocally, to return in a similar manner what they have received.

The content of exchange is not always material or as concrete as in reciprocity as simple exchange. The exchange may involve assistance on the one side and a thank you on the other. But no matter how inconsequential the content of exchange some reciprocity is expected, otherwise the other is assumed to be improperly schooled in social etiquette (reciprocal behavior). The non-reciprocal behavior is followed by a complaint like "Not even so much as a thank you."

The motivation for reciprocity as a norm is external. A person acts reciprocally because society expects it. If an individual does not act

in a reciprocal manner, society forces compliance through a variety of means including derogatory labels for behavior that is non-reciprocal, through ostracizing or through refusal by others to associate with a non-reciprocal person. Children become aware of this norm of reciprocity early in life by the way people act toward and with them and the demands (expectations for reciprocity) others make of the children. Children begin to practice reciprocity and expect others will also. Compliance to the rule of reciprocity becomes a habit and may be automatically assumed behavior. Here, the norm of reciprocity becomes "normal behavior." The practice of reciprocity leads to acceptance of reciprocity as an ideal and the appropriate way of behavior with others.

The reciprocity that occurs as a norm is often of material things, overt and easily recognizable. Personal profit does not explain the entire purpose of reciprocity as a norm therefore the overt exchange is not the entire essence of reciprocity but only the visible component. The exchange of things may have a purpose of establishing association, of linking two persons. In fact, the material exchanged may be only a medium for interaction. For example, the new boss may provide her secretary with a pretty calendar for the wall simply to signal the desire for a positive relation in the future. The content may not be as important as the process it sets in motion. The exchange of gifts in some primitive cultures acts as a medium for interaction and an overt way of setting the bond. Exchange may have the purpose of providing a friendly feeling. Exchange of material things is thus used to structure a relation. This may be its only purpose. The norm of reciprocity usually deals with externally visible exchange, even if that which is exchanged is only the medium and not the purpose of the action.

The action found with reciprocity as a norm is giving and receiving in a circular fashion. Whereas reciprocity as simple exchange was generally viewed as giving and taking with egocentric motives. Reciprocity as a norm is not entirely self-interested. There are allowances for both giving and receiving. Reciprocity is normal behavior in society; and when people interact without the presence of a profit motive (as in reciprocity as simple exchange) there is a reason for expected reciprocity. It is to one's benefit to act reciprocally because by being reciprocal, one's needs are met and so are those of the other through complementarily equal exchange. If one wants help from others, one must be willing to give help to others. One benefits because reciprocal action tends to insure future exchange.

The compulsion to reciprocity here is obligation. One complies to the norm because one must. It is expected from the partner

within the exchange and from social control structures as well. One may appeal to an outside arbitrator if reciprocity does not occur. Within reciprocity as simple exchange, there are laws of justice and external limitations but the safe guards of reciprocity as a norm are different. In simple exchange, especially in the business world, the outside arbitrator is available through legal channels and by formal application. In the competitive environment where simple exchange takes place, unequal exchange occurs only when one person is gullible and if the situation warrants it, legal action may be taken to secure actual reciprocity. In reciprocity as a norm, the outside arbitrator (society not the legal system) is observant and ready to intervene when it is felt that the situation warrants it, with or without formal request from a member of the exchanging dyad. Society (a superordinate structure) keeps watch for violators. Exploitation is thus controlled through various means (Gouldner, p. 166, 1970). Exploitation is curtailed prior to actual engagement of exchange by society's discouragement of association between unequals. Legal means may be employed also, though this is less common. (A wife sued her husband for not shoveling the sidewalk, thus causing her to fall and injure herself. She claimed that was one of his household responsibilities in exchange for his benefitting from her household duties. The court agreed with the woman.)

In some sense the golden rule is the explicit statement of the reciprocity as a norm. The golden rule suggests roles are reversible. The other is treated in a manner which would be acceptable if the roles of alter and ego were reversed. This reversibility points out the general nature of the golden rule. In its most common interpretation, the golden rule does not consider the specific other, only the general other.

The norm of reciprocity is generalizable. Reciprocity is expected in reference to everyone by all persons.

Reciprocity as a Moral Principle

Reciprocity as a moral principle is prescriptive in nature directing people to show concern for others. In some manner, then, the golden rule is also a statement of reciprocity as a moral principle for the golden rule has its roots in Christian, Jewish, and Eastern religious doctrines. As a moral principle, reciprocity is an ideal to be worked toward. It is a value (Williams, p. 134, 1973).

The reversability of roles stated by the golden rule does not give directives to assess the needs of others and meet these needs. Thus

some do not consider the golden rule a moral imperative. But others, like Weiss for example, claim the golden rule allows us to do what ought to be done (Weiss, p. 428, 1941). If this be the case the balance is shifted from specific self-interest (what can be assured for self by reciprocal behavior) to concern for the other. As such, the golden rule is similar to reciprocity as a moral principle which is not quid pro quo but contains an element of proportionality by noting the other's needs and abilities.

Reciprocity as a moral principle, unlike reciprocity as simple exchange or as a norm, is internally motivated. The internal motivation involves some elements of external pressure, though not of the legal kind. Moral behavior often responds to an ought. The actual responsive activity may be found within, but the true nature of the motivation may be compliance to standards or a reflexive, learned behavior. If either of these is the case, then, motivation can be said to be responsive, not personally initiated. But moral behavior is not merely passive compliance. Knight feels that people obey moral rules because they feel that they are right not because they should (Knight, p. 49, 1947). Kohlberg also indicates that as children move to higher levels of moral development they move away from the egocentric attitudes and behaviors of childhood and begin to internalize what they believe is morally right with less regard for the consequences of their actions (Kohlberg, 1969). Acting in accordance with a moral principle is possible through compliance to a sense of duty though generally the internally felt rightness of the principle is a combination of compliance and choice.

The development of a moral conscience is described by Piaget. The root of internal acceptance of rightness may have been obedience to demands through unilateral respect where the dictates of the other are followed through fear of the authority and through respect of judgement. As a moral conscience develops, mutual respect replaces unilateral respect and compliance, and the true virtue of reciprocal action is seen. It is this rational element which makes the response truly a moral response (Piaget, p. 382, 1965).

The rational element within reciprocity is what allows for labeling reciprocity as a moral principle as internal motivation and this is one of the things that separates it from reciprocity as a norm (although the norm cannot be said to be completely devoid of rational assent).

As a moral principle, reciprocity contains concern for the other. Simple exchange is entirely self-interested and as a norm reciprocity is partially self-interested and partially other-interested.

Meeting one's moral obligation means having a responsibility for others; being other-interested. Moral responsibility for others may be either negative or positive, a rewarding feeling may follow helping others or a feeling of guilt may follow from not accepting responsibility to help others.

The exchange within reciprocity as a moral principle may involve material things and in addition include exchanges of an abstract nature. As has been discussed, concern for the other is present in this form of reciprocity. According to MacMurray, the "full realization of moral intention can only be reached in a relation between persons in which each cares for the other" (MacMurray, p. 189, 1961). This reciprocal concern is exchanged. The concern may manifest itself as emotional support, sympathy, advice or availability. Another important abstraction exchanged is that of trust. Precisely because reciprocity is a moral injunction, and therefore will be important to others, trust is possible. "Trust as a value becomes complete only when it is reciprocal. The reciprocity produces among men a unity of a higher kind: a certainty, a stable and fixed security" (Hartmann, p. 296, 1932). It is this reciprocal trust which allows one to be confident that reciprocity is a factor in the other's action.

The condition of a lack of trust in reciprocity as simple exchange tends to provide a reciprocal action of give and take rather than an even, open system of giving and receiving. The action of reciprocity as moral principle is giving and receiving with attention directed toward the other, because morally one has responsibility for the other. The action is a continuous flowing which cannot, in theory, be stopped for breaking off relations is morally improper. Giving and receiving is a moral obligation except in the initiation stages of reciprocity. Although people are obliged to be concerned for others, the obligation is nebulous because whom one should be concerned for is not always clear. Therefore when one engages in action with a particular other rather than simply being ready to engage in action with the general other, the action is voluntary, not obligatory. The initial action of giving is voluntary; the subsequent giving and receiving is morally obligatory.

Reciprocity as a moral principle has concern directed toward the other person more than other types of reciprocity. If reversibility of roles (do unto others as you would have them do unto you) is a sufficient explanation of reciprocity as a moral principle, then, simple quid pro quo action fulfills one's moral responsibilities. All roles, however, are in reality not reversible, therefore, one's moral obligation

requires more. Morally, one may be required to give more than the other is capable of returning.

Gouldner attempts to move from the concept of reciprocity as a norm to what he calls the norm of beneficence. The norm of beneficence, he says, is found in the preaching of Christianity and requires one to give, even if the other is not capable of returning. This may mean to give something for nothing. Gouldner explains the difference between the norm of beneficence and reciprocity. The norm of reciprocity means that each has rights and obligations. The norm of beneficence creates an obligation to give but not a right to receive. Each of the two persons holds a different posture not similar ones (Gouldner, p. 263-268, 1973).

Gouldner's beneficence does not move from the realm of reciprocity as he postulates. He states quite clearly that the paradox of beneficence is that

> there is no gift that brings a *higher return* than the free gift, the gift given with no strings attached for that which is freely given truly moves men more deeply and makes them more *indebted* to their benefactors (my italics) (Gouldner, p. 277, 1973).

It is those who are well-off who can afford to give without return from others, who can afford to deal in what Gouldner claims is non-reciprocal behavior. In fact, "a reciprocity lurks in [this] behavior" of beneficence, according to Gouldner's own statement (p. 272, 1973). Beneficence is then perhaps a matter of control. The relation is not reciprocal and is only one of power of the giver over the receiver. An example of this non-reciprocal behavior can be seen with charity. The receiver of charity may need the help of another but does not appreciate the non-reciprocal nature of the relation. If something can be returned it tends to restore the reciprocal sense of interaction and thus makes the relation much more comfortable from the point of view of the recipient.

Reciprocity is anything but an attempt to control as Gouldner implies. Reciprocity as a moral principle (an ideal) works at keeping people on an equal plane.

Gouldner's concept of beneficence involves, in some ways, reciprocity as a moral principle. Beneficence is other-concerned when it is truly altruistic. It is not simply quid pro quo behavior. It goes beyond rights to the needs of the other. It, therefore, goes beyond the norm of reciprocity to reciprocity as a moral principle.

Reciprocity requires justice. True justice is not a balanced scale but must make allowances for variations in needs and abilities. Reciprocal exchange must include proportionality otherwise the exchange is not moral. Proportionality assesses differences in abilities, needs and resources and balances the scales by moving the fulcrum rather than demanding equal weight on both sides. It is reciprocity in terms of proportionality that constitutes the bond of association in mutual exchange (Aristotle, p. 124-25, 1962).

The proportionality is formal. It assumes some uniformity of human preferences. Reciprocity as a moral principle does not meet particular desires but is constrained to general ways of interaction. The specific desires of the unique other are not directly a part of reciprocity as a moral principle as they are in reciprocity as intimate exchange.

Reciprocity as Intimate Exchange

A brief outline of reciprocity of intimate exchange will complete the comparison of five different forms of reciprocity. A more extensive explanation is found in the next chapter.

Reciprocity as intimate exchange is internal and voluntary. The content of exchange in this form of reciprocity includes material and abstract things. The motion of reciprocity as intimate exchange is giving and receiving. It is a smooth circular action which encompasses the two within a relationship. There may be expectations and demands due to the difficulty in perceiving and meeting the other's needs. Asking may be a part of reciprocity as intimate exchange.

If reciprocity as intimate exchange fails to function it disrupts the interaction between the two. If the breakdown continues over a long period of time, it may dissolve the relationship. The outward presentation of the relationship may remain as a shell but the dynamic aspect of the relationship is destroyed when reciprocity is absent.

Reciprocity provides for all the rewarding features of friendship. The material aspects allow a medium for association and for assistance for each friend. The abstract aspects provide rewards in and of themselves.

Reciprocity as intimate exchange is specific and personalized. There is no external control. Other forms of reciprocity involve a generalized nature. As intimate exchange, reciprocity does not apply to others but only to *this one person*. It is direct and appropriate, meeting the other's needs.

Summary

These five forms of reciprocity are not a developmental sequence. Although the egocentric child does move from reciprocity based on desire for personal gain to reciprocity based on moral concern, the adult is involved in many forms of reciprocity. These different forms arise according to the situation and the people involved. One form may be more appropriate to one situation than another. Reciprocity as intimate exchange is not the ultimate of reciprocity but rather a form appropriate in certain situations.

All of these forms overlap to a degree, with other forms. In human action, they all are mixed together in the various dealings with others. Most often people do not associate with others, certainly in ongoing relationships, with only one form of reciprocity.

Reciprocity is learned in early stages of life where the proclaimed value of reciprocity becomes more clear through practice and additional practice improves one's ability at reciprocity. One does not become reciprocal and remain so. Reciprocity varies in kind, degree, and intensity. Reciprocity is never complete. In addition, people are capable, at times, of being more or less able to to engage in reciprocal action. Reciprocity is a value and something that people must work toward as well as something to practice.

Chapter 7

Reciprocity in Friendship: Content and Process

"Friendship...is inconceivable without reciprocity."
Ignace Lepp, p. 33, 1966

Reciprocity is the essence of friendship. Reciprocal interaction between people who care for each other is the means of, and ultimate purpose for, friendship. The reciprocity that makes friendship is partly all of the types of reciprocity described in the previous chapter. It may be at one time simple exchange, at another it may be moral reciprocity or mixtures of several of these. In addition it involves a type of exchange different from any other form of reciprocity. This form can be called reciprocity as intimate exchange. It is not solely that intimate exchange is of a sacred nature, although it sometimes is, but that the exchange is unique to the two friends alone.

Reciprocity as intimate exchange can be found in all intimate relationships including kinship, blood or marriage, lovers or friends as described herein. It is exclusive to intimate relationships with the exception of the I-Thou relationship which Buber discusses so eloquently (Buber, 1970).

Reciprocity as intimate exchange can exist between spouses, lovers, parents and children, yet it may in fact be absent from such relationships. When an element of loving concern between assumed equals is missing so is reciprocity as intimate exchange, though reciprocity of other forms may be present. This discussion of reciprocity in friendship will include intimate relationships which could be categorized under other personal or kinship relationship labels as well.

Reciprocity as Intimate Exchange

Phillips characterizes an intimate relationship as one which has a high degree and variety of exchange. Intimacy involves regular exchanges of "goods, services, advice, time, support, and other sentiments" (Phillips, p. 283, 1976). In friendship, the closeness allows more fruitful reciprocity whereas formal relations keep too much distance decreasing the reciprocity possible (deVries, p. 12, 1968). Reciprocity in friendship is inclusive allowing the most ways for the dynamics of giving and receiving. It allows a forum for a unique and special reciprocity not found elsewhere in other relations.

In any association reciprocity varies in degree, intensity, and appearance. Within friendship, it can be said that reciprocity is always present although it may appear to be missing from an isolated moment. Because a friendship is a relationship with a past and a future, it is not always possible to isolate the reciprocity in a moment of time. The actual giving/receiving and giving/receiving may be difficult to see in the complete cycle. The cycle does not simply circle round and round. The movement is much more complex with different segments functioning interdependently.

Reciprocity as intimate exchange is internally motivated. There is no external imposition of what ought to be. This is especially true in America where friendship is not directed or supported by society. Therefore society has little to say regarding the dynamics of friendship (unless there are flagrant distortions). According to Suttles, one of friendship's characteristics is that it allows deviation from the norm (Suttles, p. 132-3, 1970). People act from mutual cooperation in friendship, and do what works for them not what is right according to an external authority, thus interaction possibilities are greatly increased.

The reciprocity is voluntary. Mauss points out that personal exchange involves spontaneity which suggests a free giving. Friendship is a voluntary association and the dynamics of friendship are also of a voluntary nature. But Mauss also says that exchange includes obligation (p. 63, 1967). These two statements appear to be in contradiction. An obligation for reciprocity as intimate exchange is not a norm which is a societal prescriptive, rather it is a personal expectation. As deVries notes, reciprocity is a more easily accepted principle when there is a working together voluntarily (p. 13, 1968). In other words, reciprocity is needed for relation but when a relation is voluntary the need for reciprocity is not onerous. The expectation for reciprocity is not a burdensome thing. Rubin says once a relationship has developed the degree of self-interest and other-interest changes (p. 86, 1973). Concern for the other moves one toward a desire to give to the other. The reciprocity is not as in simple exchange which provides only for economic self-gain.

Reciprocity as intimate exchange is personal and subjective. It involves a concern for the specific other, not a concern for the general other as in reciprocity as a norm. The specific other must be dealt with as a unique and special person whose needs, abilities, interests are not the same as anyone else's. The other is a subject, not an object. Reversibility of roles cannot meet the necessary requirements for reciprocity in friendship. Friendship is not a relationship of roles. It is a relationship of persons. One must meet the other as a unique non-

reproducible person and through awareness, communication, intuition, and empathy act reciprocally with this particular person.

Reciprocity as intimate exchange is also a private affair. Others may not see it or understand it or find it relevant to them. The friends are the only two who need to find the reciprocity fulfilling.

The reciprocity in friendship may be difficult to see even by those involved. The difficulty stems from the complexity and also from the abstract nature of the exchange. It may be only an emotional exchange. From the outside, the behavior manifested by these feelings is extremely hard to decipher. From within the relationship, there may be little conscious awareness of what the content of the abstract exchange really is and what its effects are.

The Process of Reciprocity in Friendship

In reciprocity as intimate exchange there is both a giving and receiving. The suffix *ing* as in "giving" connotes the dynamic aspect of this action. Reciprocity must have the two aspects of giving and receiving, yet it is not a back and forth motion between two persons, which would be disjointed. Observe two children playing catch. One gives, the other receives, yet there is not a stopping and starting but a constant motion. The game consists of the giving and receiving and although there is a pause in the motion of the ball as it moves between the two, there is no pause in the motion of what is necessary to keep the ball moving. This example shows the constant and circular motion of the giving and receiving in friendship. If, as with the children, one gives and the other takes, it is not reciprocity.

One must receive and accept a gift and receive the significance that it has. Buber explains the distinction between taking and receiving. "He who takes what is given him and does not experience it as a gift is not really receiving; and so the gift turns into theft." One must know, according to Buber, not only what is given but the giver, for it is a personal gift which includes not only the content but also the spirit of the giver (Buber, p. 143, 1966).

Giving and receiving are both essential. Taking without any action of giving is stealing. Receiving from another without giving in return is actually taking or exploitation. If the receiving is missing, there is also an inequality established. Giving and refusing to receive (whether advertently or inadvertently) is self-interested and puts the giver in control (MacMurray, p. 189, 1961; Cotroneo, p. 4-5, n.d.). This control is maintained by always keeping the other indebted. It makes an unequal relation. It tends to cause discomfort (and it does not

always allow an easy exit from the relationship). It is not unlike charity, where an inequality is established placing the receiver in an obsequious position.

The giving and receiving is circular and continues in friendship. It is not abrupt giving and returning but rather an ongoing giving. A friendship contains an ongoing aspect as it is a relationship with a future. Once the initial giving and receiving has occurred, future giving and receiving is accomplished more easily. This applies similarity when there is different content of exchange, the initial exchange of one type facilitates the future exchanges.

The circularity of the reciprocity can expand the original meaning of the relationship. Frank explains this circularity in lov*ing*, which unlike love, is dynamic.

> We begin to see that if a person is loveable, we put loveableness into them, we invest them with special qualities that we delight to behold and then act toward them as loveable, hoping to evoke reciprocally their loving response. If we are fortunate we establish a "virtuous circle" (as contrasted with a "vicious circle") where the more we impute loveableness to another and act toward him or her as loveable the more that person becomes loving toward us (Frank, p. 32, 1953).

There is a spiraling effect inherent in reciprocity which strengthens the relationship.

This circular giving and receiving encompasses the two within the reciprocity. Once the relationship has developed, the two, as friends, are found within a field of reciprocity. It is this encompassing aspect which tends to continue the relationship sometimes without conscious effort.

Reciprocity is an intricate interwoven giving and receiving. It is not an action-reaction. Williams explains that reciprocity is a principle of give and take where the nature of the give depends in part on the nature of the take and subsequent give (p. 50, 1973). There is an interlocking between the giving and receiving.

The two do not become a single unit in their interaction. They remain distinct in order to coordinate. DePaoli explains this together-yet-separate issue as "a life of partnership among persons who are friends" characterized by their mutual interdependence where "the persons who are united in a loving relationship of this type are reflected

entities whose self-identities are dialectically intertwined" (DePaoli, p. 223, 1971).

Reciprocity is action with another, yet action compatible with the freedom of the person. Reciprocity prevents exploitation. The most developed form of reciprocity according to Gould requires that

> a) each agent consciously recognizes the other as free, that is, as individualized and differentiated, and as capable of self-realization; and b) each acts with respect to the other in ways which enhance the other's agency on the basis of a consideration of the other's needs and c) both agents take such mutual enhancement of each other's agency as a conscious aim (Gould, p. 41-2, 1977).

This atmosphere of "full reciprocity" then provides for the potentials of each and enhances the development of each.

In an isolated reciprocal moment, the content of giving and receiving is not a simple tit for tat. With reciprocity as a norm there is reversibility of roles in determining the return appropriate. But role associations are not friendships. Reversing roles does not consider the question of the unique and personal needs of a friend.

Levinas has criticized the concept of reciprocity in close relationships because there is no "interchangeability" of positions (Levinas, p. 146, 1967). But in the personal relationship of friendship the other is more fully understood than in other relations. A friend is not the same as oneself. The knowledge of one's friend reveals a person with different needs and abilities and therefore reveals the inappropriateness of interchangeability of roles.

Aristotle, an early proponent of reciprocity, states that "in perfect and complete friendship...each should receive in all matters what he gives the other, in the same or in similar form; that is what friends should be able to count on" (Aristotle, p. 221, 1962). Similar form need not be giving to the other something of equal material value. It might be more possible and appropriate to give emotionally for something of material value which has been received.

Kurth describes the differences between the distributive justice of social exchange, in friendship, and in less intimate relationships. Whereas friends assume future association (and have a history of association), acquaintances can not rely on that. Friends therefore have a basis for allowing exchange to even out over the course of the relationship. Immediate parity is not essential. Friends have "standing accounts" (Kurth, p. 163, 1970). Equal return is not imperative in

friendship according to Davis. Davis points out that, in fact, equal return is an insult by making a close relationship into an "economic" situation rather than using a rule of "approximate reciprocity" (Davis, p. 360, 1973).

Friendship is voluntary and so is the reciprocity found within it. Friendship has, then, no general rules of what is appropriate. Rather reciprocity must be sensitive to the present and unique situation of the friend. In friendship, giving must take into account the needs of this unique other. The abilities and resources and limitations of the giver are also important considerations.

Weinstein has shown that friends are willing to allow indebtedness, to permit an inequality to remain. Weinstein's study created a situation of inequality. Friends were comfortable with crediting the other with some superior abilities. In stranger dyads, the persons acted as if the inequality was not present or tried to reverse the roles and allow the inferior to be the superior. Within friendship dyads, the persons of inferior abilities acknowledged the others' superior positions with praise and thanks and the pair continued to function in positions which reflected the established superior and inferior roles. The strangers needed to repay the superior with taking on a role of leadership but friends could allow momentary inequity to stand in this particular situation because future relating would permit reciprocation (Weinstein et al., 1969).

The Content of Exchange in Friendship

In friendship, the process is the ongoing giving and receiving which involves an intricate weave of giver and receiver. The content may or may not have a real significance of its own. It may be only a medium for relationship. A weekly luncheon date, for example, may not have important content but can serve as a time for the friends to be together. It is a support of the bond. In realms of the emotional, social, or psychological, that which is exchanged may be very valuable for the development of the individuals.

There are many different categories of content of exchange. An exchange of material things may be easily witnessed but exchange on an emotional level, for example, may be visible only through the behavior it causes. One may have respect for a friend but this feeling or emotion may not be recognized unless it is given some outward sign such as speech although an intuitive sense of the emotional is possible within a close relationship.

Reciprocity in friendship includes all forms of reciprocity. Materials exchanged may be merely a convenience (although an expected convenience) but not the real crux of the relationship. Davis explains this well.

> If the economics of intimacy constitutes the substructure of personal relations for close friends, at least, it is a phenomenologically invisible one. Should it surface in their consciousness at all, they would consider their relationship breaking down (Davis, p. 166, 1973).

Material things can intrude on the closeness of the relationship. In reality, exchange of material things is much less complex because it is overt and value is easily assessed but a problem arises in that material things can become entirely objective. That is, trading one thing for another with a friend may exclude the spirit of the friendship within the transaction. Material things may lose the subjective nature of the other, a necessity in intimate exchange. When material exchange becomes important, the relationship tends to become objective.

Exchange can occur on an intellectual level. Exchange of ideas may arise in order to develop a better understanding or it may act only as a medium for interaction. The content of the conversation may be only a vehicle or it may be pertinent to the relationship.

The intellectual realm can involve exchange of influence. In friendship, this influence is not generally for the purpose of persuasion (to win the other over to one's own way of thinking), for such a competitive attitude is incongruent with friendship. As Buber says

> The desire to influence the other, then, does not mean the effort to change the other, to inject one's own "rightness" into him; but it means the effort to let that which is recognized as right, as just, as true...through one's influence take seed and grow in the form suited to individuation (Buber, p. 69, 1965b).

In intellectual exchange, it is obvious that exchanging like for like is not of much use. Intellectual exchange may be an exchange of information but it is more likely to be a chance to share and develop ideas more fully. It may be easier to share half-baked or far-fetched schemes with a friend. The risk is less. A friend is willing to listen

nonjudgementally; together the two can investigate and build on one another's ideas. Intellectual exchange is a good example of the synergetic development that can occur through reciprocity.

Reciprocity occurs on an emotional level in friendship but emotions are even more ephemeral than other items of exchange in friendship. Emotions are visible through behavioral manifestations or symbols used to represent these feelings. It must be kept in mind that as with other forms of reciprocity, emotional exchange is not evenly balanced on both sides.

Appreciation is often reciprocated in like manner. It may also be given in reference to any number of things received from a friend including material things, gifts, or the presence of the other. Appreciation is generally visible as a "thank you," a gift, a smile or other symbols. According to Simmel, appreciation goes beyond a repayment for a task or gift. We do not thank someone only for what he or she does but for what he or she is (Simmel, p. 389, 1964).

Observable reciprocal concern is a common place occurrence. The expression "Hello, how are you?" is a form of greeting in this culture. It is most often met with an automatic response, usually of a positive nature such as "Fine, how are you?" This greeting is extended liberally to all, whether he or she is greatly or minimally valued. Within friendship, a note of real reciprocal concern may be placed in these little phrases. With a friend, the question is real and intends to update the knowledge of one friend about the other. The real depth of concern for a friend goes beyond verbal inquiry. A friend is attentive and notices changes in behavior which give indications of the other's present state. A friend is someone who cares for you. This care must be reciprocal for the relationship to exist.

Responsibility follows from concern. If one is truly concerned about a friend, some responsibility is taken for the friend's welfare. There is no clear-cut division of responsibility in friendship, yet it involves a willingness to help, to give, and to care for one's friend. Responsibility also must be reciprocal.

Another abstraction of reciprocal exchange in friendship is that of trust. Trust or confidence is given. It can not be requested. Trust in another acts both as a statement of respect and honor and as a demand that the trust is justified. Trust must be met by a justification for that trust. The trustful person stakes him or herself against the trustworthiness of the other. But since trust is such a high honor to bestow upon another, trust is compelling and is usually met with trustworthiness. Trust needs to be exchanged in kind. "Trust as a value becomes complete only when it is reciprocal," according to Hartmann and Simmel (Hartmann, p. 292, 1932; Simmel, p. 348, 1964).

Love is given and received by friends. Unreciprocal or unrequited love is a common topic because it is so painful and so unnatural. One-way love is sometimes called admiration, awe, or worship but if real love is to persist, it needs to be reciprocal. Loving another tends to evoke loving from the other. The movement of love in a reciprocal manner tends to cause an increase in the amount of love.

Affection is often the physical manifestation of love (although affection can be exchanged in situations of liking rather than the stronger bond of love). Affection is generally freely given. One gives a kiss, a hug, a smile, a pat on the head. These are, in addition, often reciprocated in kind. A smile elicits a smile or a hug elicits a simultaneous return of a hug. The representation of love through the signs of affection may be more easily seen than other emotional exchanges yet it does not give a clear statement of degree or intensity of the felt emotion. Sometimes a more explicit statement of emotional caring is given.

Reciprocity as intimate exchange may be found in the psychological realm. Acceptance and affirmation must be reciprocal in personal encounter, otherwise one is denying him or herself respect by being in a debilitating situation. Acceptance and affirmation are psychological supports for a friend and provide him or her with an atmosphere which permits growth and development.

Self-disclosure is found also to occur in a reciprocal fashion. There are two reasons for this. Jourard's research indicates "Disclosure invites or begets disclosure" (Jourard, p. 13, 1971). That is, because one is willing to disclose something about him or herself, the other feels compelled to do likewise. Also disclosure acknowledges the presence of trust. If one is trusted, she or he generally trusts and will be willing to disclose as well. Disclosure is appropriate when it is reciprocal. It is this self-disclosure according to Rubin, that moves people from acquaintanceship toward friendship (Rubin, p. 163, 1973). Disclosure allows one to show trust and confidence in the other. It encourages the relationship to grow because of this trust and because the pair have more common knowledge. Disclosure allows the person to learn about him or herself and test out reactions in the safe environment of friendship. We come to know ourselves through others MacMurray says (p. 169, 1961). Disclosing one's self is in addition, giving of one's self to a friend. As Camus notes, in disclosing to those we love "we are no longer revealing ourselves in order to seem [as we might with acquaintances] but in order to give" (Camus as cited by Luft, p. 132, 1969).

The Spirit of Exchange

The way that material things are exchanged in friendship is different than in other relations even though the content may be the same. If one gives the use of the car or a tool to a friend, the spirit of exchange is different than if the same things had been given to an acquaintance. It is rewarding to be able to provide for material needs of a friend. These material things are given freely and thus it is easier for a friend to receive.

The spirit of exchange is most easily seen in the gift. Gifts are given to good friends, but rarely to acquaintances with exceptions found in the social norms of our culture. Thus the gift generally signifies the value of the relationship. The gift is freely given. The gift given to acknowledge a birthday or holiday is perhaps an expectation to be filled yet friends use these occasions to signify the bond between them. The spontaneous gift, given "without reason," no matter how insignificant in monetary value is imbued with the value the friend holds in the heart of the giver.

Gifts are often of material form but they possess a definite subjective nature. It is, in fact, not the value of the gift but the spirit of the gift that is relevant. Mauss's anthropological work, *The Gift*, insists that in primitive cultures, the exchange of material things in the form of gifts has a purpose far beyond economic utility. Material exchanges are important to the economics of living but also are essential in establishing bonds of association. Because these materials were not reduced to common denominators, such as money, they maintained a subjective nature. By exchanging gifts, rather than paying for material items with a common token of exchange, primitives exchange a part of themselves, for each gift contains part of the giver (Mauss, 1967).

Guitton poses a theological position regarding exchange and its meaning. Things exist for the purpose of relation and they have been given to man by God, according to Guitton, in order to be exchanged because in the course of the exchanging, love will be increased (Guitton, 1966).

Gifts move beyond economic value. The gift is a vehicle of love, a sign of love. The gift incorporates the spirit of the giver. The material gift acts as a sign of the feelings involved in the relationship. It is according to Johann, only through these signs (gifts) of love that the Thou is present to the I (Johann, p. 48, 1966). Although it is true that visible signs are more easily perceived, it does not follow that there are no means of perception other than visual therefore the presence of the Thou may be discovered through other senses.

Gifts need not be of material form to be real. It can be that the giving and receiving of reciprocity in friendship is exchange of feelings. Feelings are a person's internal state and they are also the heart of one's attitude of the other. Feelings are not only the underlying fact of loving but also a means of interpersonal communication. Feelings find expression in outward manifestations. They are not hidden only within the internal workings of an individual. Through these expressions, there is communication between friends. Sadler states that the feelings "open the world of creative exchange which otherwise was neither visible nor possible" (Sadler, p. 196, 1969).

Feelings spill out the willingness, the desire, for this relationship. Feelings can be expressed in the form of material gifts, or through verbal expression, a sign of affection, or even in the presence of one's self with the other.

A gift includes the spirit of the giver. It has part of the giver within it. A friend gives him or herself, through his or her presence to the other. It is only this presence which permits exchange and dialogue. Sadler explains this presence and its importance in exchange. The reality of presence asks

> "are you with me." If the question is genuinely asked
> and the answer is genuinely, "Yes, I am with you,"
> the two persons discover that there has been an
> exchange as in an act of sharing which has involved
> them in a total way. Marcel describes this presence
> as a phenomenon which reveals an exchange of free
> acts; it is a mutual response which signifies to me
> that the other person is not placed there in front of me
> but that we transcend external spatiality in a personal
> reality of sharing (Sadler, p. 112, 1969).

This spatiality of which Sadler speaks is the place of friendship, it is in Buber's terminology "the between," that part of the relationship formed and bounded by reciprocity.

The motion of reciprocity as intimate exchange has been described as a giving and receiving occurring together rather than response of one to the other. Guitton explains this unique sense of temporality and spatiality of love in a reciprocal relationship:

> Loving and being loved are one and the same act: the
> gift which is being made includes the very being of
> the giver in its indivisible totality; it is the gift not

so much of what *one has* as of what *one is* (Guitton, p. 81, 1966).

Both loving and being loved are present within a reciprocal moment. Together, the two friends are within the reciprocity of this love.

Summary

Reciprocity in an intimate relationship like that of close friendship is particularistic as Foa and Foa noted. Experiencing this reciprocity is different than the experiencing of reciprocal interaction with non-personal relationships. Both the kinds of resources and the spirit of the exchange vary because of the attributes of the relationship within which these exchanges occur.

Chapter 8

Friendship Today

The fact that Americans are interested in friendship is undeniable but why they are interested is not totally clear. Is friendship of concern simply because it is a relationship that is different from most other relations in which people engage, or because its clandestine nature makes it exciting, or because it is a relationship based entirely on choice, or because of the realized and/or expected benefits? Who are the people who invest in making and keeping friends?

Influential Factors in Initiating and Maintaining Friendships

Americans have long been criticized as being stiff and unfriendly but Americans are not without friends nor do they wish to be. However, Americans are perhaps more concerned with their individuality than their European counterparts. Americans strive for homes off in the country away from others; clamor for personal space and privacy in their homes and at work. These things do separate people and decrease friendship possibilities.

Very few people are entirely without some sort of friend, however. Even those who are not popular usually stick together with others like themselves. The recluse is very uncommon, the inability to make friends itself being a criteria indicative of poor mental health. Even when we feel we have few friends we are reticent to acknowledge it to anyone including ourselves.

What creates the variance between the apparent friendless and gregarious? People who have a great number of friends are likely to have less restive qualifications for friendship, desire relationships more, work at relationships more readily, or combinations of these things. Personality is certainly a dominant factor in making and valuing friends. Research indicates that people who are identified as lonely have "greater passivity, a lack of assertiveness, greater shyness and self consciousness...[and] difficulty in making friends naturally and with ease" (Jones, Hansson, and Cutrona, p. 145-6, 1984). Some people simply have very high expectations, thus decreasing those acceptable as friends (Naegele, 1958).

There are a number of circumstances beyond shyness and lack of social skills that also seem to influence the number of friends people have. Age, socio-economic status, marital status, family and job responsibilities, and gender are all variables that influence investments people make in developing and keeping friends.

Differences in an individual's ability and desire to form friendships varies with age. Early socialization for friendship is a salient factor in later interest in friendship. But factors such as previous success in friendship formation and the type of people who actually become friends influence future friendship.

Developmental theory sheds some light on variations in seeking out and succeeding at friendships. Children are very egocentric and have not yet developed certain cognitive abilities according to Piaget thus they don't exhibit some of the characteristics considered common in adult friendship (Piaget, 1965). Children's friendships may therefore go unnoticed because they are different from what is expected. The psychologist, Harry Stack Sullivan discussed the importance of childhood friendship fifty years ago but more specific study is finally beginning to take place today.

Recent evidence suggests that even infants and toddlers gain from relationships with others their own age. Little friends provide a means of social comparison thus facilitating identity formation, and providing a sense of belonging (Rubin, p. 4-6, 1980). Little friends learn things from their peers that are not available to them from parents or other older individuals. Lewis suggests that infants show a "cluster of specific and particular interactions with familiar infants" and that these relations are different from those the infants would have with others unfamiliar to them or with older individuals (Lewis, p. 58, 1975). Little children are capable of, and often do develop good friendships. They often play with one child when others are available, indicating definite preferences. Social development is enhanced by friendship with others even as a child (Dickens and Perlman, p. 103, 1987). Furman begins his article on children's friendship this way:

> Positive peer relations are an important part of
> children's social networks that are now recognized to
> be as essential for healthy adaptation as positive
> parent-child relations are. In particular, the egalitarian
> nature of positive peer relations appears to foster
> moral development, the control of aggression, the
> acquisition of norms and values, and emotional and
> social development (p. 103, 1984).

Unfortunately the lack of control infants and small children have over
their environments may mean their relationships are easily terminated.

The various stages of cognitive and social development that
the individual traverses from infancy through adulthood produce different
abilities and needs in the friendship realm. Adolescents, for example,
have advanced cognitively and socially and are less self-centered yet their
predominant need according to Erikson is a search for identity (Erikson,
p. 260-2, 1963). The influence of development of friendship formation
is not unidirectional but rather as Dickens and Perlman suggest,
friendship formation influences the general development of the
individual child (p. 94, 1981). Thus with children, adolescents, and
even adults, the friendships people experience influence their future
relations as well as their personal development.

Age and related life circumstances influence friendship
formation. "Middle-aged and high school groups" had the fewest friends
in one study of friendship across the life cycle (Lowenthal, Thurnher,
and Chiriboga, p. 49, 1979). In another study, the middle span of
adulthood had the greatest social contact (Hess, 1972). Younger adults
were more likely involved with friends than other age groups according
to Palsi and Ransford (p. 256, 1987). Multiple interactive variables
seem to better account for differences between age distinguished
friendships, with young, unmarried, and childless people having more
involvement with friends (Palsi and Ransford, p. 256, 1987).

By the time people reach midlife they seem to want to hold
onto their friends (Fox, Gibbs, and Auerbach, p. 496, 1985). They
may work harder to maintain existing friendships. Several factors
associated with advancing age tend to influence the number of friends
older people have.

Older people may have lost friends because of high mobility in
this culture and through death of friends. Physical and economic
constraints may prohibit maintaining existing friendships or building
new ones. "A consistent finding across studies...is that the frequency of
contact with friends declines as people get older" (Dickens and Perlman,

p. 110, 1987). The quality of friendship may vary with age as well. Friendships in later life are maintained and appreciated often because of their duration whereas friends of younger people are dependent on common roles for development and maintenance (Hess, 1972). "The value of friends may actually increase in later life as family and career responsibilities diminish....[it appears that] older adults prefer existing friends rather than newer ones" (Shea, Thompson, and Blieszner, p. 83, 1988). Retirement itself seems to strengthen the friendship people have (Lowenthal, Thurnher, and Chiriboga, 1977). This is likely due to change in responsibilities and more available time.

Economic status and perhaps the related issues of job demands seem to influence friendships. Lower socio-economic status may allow less opportunity at least for more distant relationships (Palsi and Ransford, p. 257, 1987). The importance one places on career and demands of one's job also plays a part. For example, Myron Brenton found that high level managers had a difficult time forming close friendships. They attributed this inability to the fact that they were constantly in a competitive struggle which left little room for relationships. Their interest was focused on work (Brenton, 1974). Brenton notes further support for his contention of men's difficulty with friendship formation in the Harvard study of business people which indicated many business men cared for others but were unable to express affection which in turn curtailed their relationships (Brenton, 1974).

Marital status causes variation in attention to friendships. However, Tschann notes that "In spite of the potential importance of marital status, research assessing its impact on friendship has been relatively sparse" (p. 67, 1988). She goes on to say that her evidence indicates marriage is associated with quality declines in friendships for men; this is not true for women (p. 77, 1988). Tschann suggests that it is possible that women's intimacy needs are not completely met by spouses (Tschann, p. 79, 1988). There are indications that intimate friendships between women are "the most open, the most comfortable, the most supportive, the most reciprocal, the most mature relationships" women have and these close friendships sustain women in their other relationships including those with spouses (Safilios-Rothschild, p. 380, 1981). Perhaps friendships co-existing with marriage are more important to women than to men.

There has been considerable investigation of gender differences in friendship (Wright, 1982 and 1988; Fox, Gibbs, and Auerbach, 1985; Sapadin, 1988; Bell, 1981; Fischer and Narus, 1981). Carol Gilligan's often cited work, *In a different voice*, holds that women focus more on relationships and are willing to sacrifice more for the

maintenance of all kinds of relationships than men (1982). Women make significant, emotional investments in friends, producing fuller, more intense relationships (Booth, 1972; Lowenthal, 1977; Bell, 1981a). Women seem to have more personalized concern and knowledge about their friends than men (Wright, 1982). One study that measured outcomes from friendship found women's friendships to be more intimate than men's (Fischer and Narus, p. 453, 1981).

Women's friendships have also been found to be more emotionally based than men's (Bell, p. 417, 1981a). Women disclose more intimate topics than men (Tschann, 1988). Another study indicated "women of all ages were more expressive in their friendship showing higher levels of empathy and altruism than men" (Fox, Gibbs, and Auerbach, p. 489, 1985). And men's intimate friendships were less personal and intimate than women's (Sapadin, p. 388, 1988).

Past experiences of friendship are likely to influence future investment. If women's ways of being focus on relationships as Gilligan indicates, than it would be expected that women would be more attentive to friendships. The research seems to support this notion. According to Hays (1989) women also indicate greater satisfaction is derived with same sex friends than men (p.36). If individuals are comfortable reaching out to others and experience friendship as rewarding, they are likely to continue with such relationships, maintaining those already formed and initiating new relationships.

The Value of Friendship

Friendship is a rewarding association although it has been noted that the benefits incumbent are not the motives for the development of strong, long lasting, friendships. The basis of a friendship seems to spring up before a purpose or direction for the particular relationship is even considered. There are far more rewards than casual reflection would suggest. There is much pain, hurt, frustration, anger, fear, and anxiety present in friendship precisely because of its import. But the presence of these negative emotions does not by any means repudiate the general goodness inherent in friendship. The resiliency of friendship in spite of problems attests to the value of the relationship. Friendship's benefits range from economic and social rewards to more subjective rewards of a psychological nature.

A most obvious benefit of friendship is the pleasure it produces. The pleasure is likely to be present in the getting acquainted

stages of the relationship. This may be part of the reason for the beginnings of the friendship. It is fun to do things with others and mundane activities take on a special air with a friend. Joys are increased when shared.

A friend can be useful, lending another a cup of sugar or money or helping with repairs to the house, lending the car or doing errands. These are all matters of utility. It is with a close relationship that one knows he or she can make use of the other without using him or her. A friend is glad to be useful. C.S. Lewis poses eloquently the manner of a friend's giving.

> The stereotyped "Don't mention it" here expresses what we really feel. The mark of perfect friendship is not that help will be given when a pinch comes (of course it will) but that, having been given it makes no difference at all (Lewis, p. 102, 1960).

It is, according to Lewis, a horrible waste of good time together for real friends to have to hash over this helpfulness and subsequent thankfulness.

In addition to the normal material things that can be given or exchanged in friendship, there are such things as time and energy, very important commodities in today's world.

According to Reis (1984) there is a great deal of acceptance of the premise that "social support is an important element in the prevention and treatment of illness" (p. 21). But as Reis points out there have been difficulties in correlational studies of social support which have not produced results indicating an "understanding of *why* and *how* social support has beneficial effects" (p. 21). In considering what friendship can be it is reasonable to consider what benefits can be found within it.

The psychological benefits of friendship are often subtle and sublime, yet such benefits are much more difficult to acquire outside of friendship. Whereas material benefits of friendship can likely be purchased in the common market and even affection can be found in friendly relations, many psychological benefits do not appear without an atmosphere of friendship.

Material and informational benefits are more blatant. People can give objects or services without exceptional involvement. Yet the benefits may be of a more subjective nature, actually found in the relationship itself. When benefits are subjective they are less discernible as and less accessible to verbalization. This elusive quality

does not project the import of the benefits. Friendship is an enormous force in the psychological growth of a person.

The volitional nature of friendship is one reason for its great impact on a person's security, as one does not have to be a friend. Thus it is that much more important that he or she is a friend. Wiseman describes the impact of volition in friendship well.

> The friendship bond is basically fragile. At the crux ...[is the] continuous pull between intimacy and commitment on the one hand and voluntary association and freedom of behaviour on the other....[but] friends do manage the balancing act for which the position calls. They do maintain stability of perceived personality and behaviour; they do fulfill expectations a great deal of the time; they do not overdo demands. They do forgive friends who fail to meet unnegotiated contract expectations. Perhaps, because of feelings bordering on euphoria which they experience in the presence of a close friend, they do see it as all worthwhile (p. 210, 1986).

Friends are people who are trusted and respected. Being able to discuss a troublesome situation with a friend provides a safe environment to let out all fears and to have them accepted as fears rather than scoffed at as unimportant. Together, in this atmosphere, friends can discuss alternatives and see situations in a new light. The other can provide a different perspective. Counsel can be useful to the other whether it is actually heeded or not. It allows one to move to new and different levels of understanding just through discussion.

A friend can broaden another's world through vicarious experiences. And in experiencing things together friends can share thoughts and feelings. The shared learning is greater than the learnings of the two persons individually. A friend can encourage one to step further into new ventures, try new areas, and explore new talents. This is done through suggestion, challenge, through support, encouragement, and praise.

Friendship can be beneficial because two can maintain a higher level of energy than one, for each takes a turn in being the impetus. "It is not easy to be continuously active by oneself," says Aristotle, "it is easier in the company of and in relation to others" (Aristotle, p. 265, 1962). "It is the function of our friends to turn us on...." (Greeley, p. 110, 1971). A friend challenges you to be more and better and with the

support and care freely given, it is easier for the person to move toward success.

A friend is admired and respected and thus friends can act as role models. One may set out to emulate characteristics of a friend or one may begin to develop such qualities through association without conscious attention. In a way, then, a friend is the hero-like character so salient in the continued reshaping of the vital, growing person.

Greeley describes how the relationship itself is beneficial.

> There is an electricity about a friendship relationship. We are both more relaxed and more sensitive, more confident and more vulnerable, more creative and more reflective, more energetic and more casual, more excited and more serene. It is as though when we come in contact with our friend we enter into a different environment where the air we breathe is more pure, the sounds we hear are sharper, the colors we see more dramatic, and the ideas we think quicker and more insightful. The physical environment, of course, is not different at all, but the psycho-social environment is completely different, because now we are in a situation not only where we are free to be ourselves but where we have no choice (Greeley, p. 110, 1971).

The atmosphere of the relationship so vividly described by Greeley can be a catalyst. And as Greeley suggests, friendship encourages the unique characteristics of the individual to develop. The other is not only accepted by his or her friend but also confirmed. This confirmation to Buber is not just agreement with the other but affirmation of the present or potential of a friend. Buber described the I-Thou relationship which is like experiences of friendship. He says "The inmost growth of self...[occurs] between men...in the mutuality of making present...together with the mutuality of acceptance, of affirmation and confirmation" (Buber, p. 71, 1965). Because the self is accepted as real and worthwhile, the person may feel reassured and confident.

There is a cathartic aspect to friendship for its acceptance allows release of emotions. A misshapen or poorly focused aspect of self can be let out with the confidence that it will be accepted and thus dealt with productively. Because there is a mutuality of self-disclosure, one is freer to let out the more bizarre characteristics of him or herself

which otherwise are kept carefully hidden, often at some cost of energy and psychological well being.

A friend can act as a mirror for awareness and understanding for the other. By testing out oneself with a friend there is an safe sounding board. Only another personality can be a counter-pole. Hartmann feels that love permits one to be "for himself" rather than "in himself." As he describes it "Personal love is a value complimentary to personality, a communication to it of its own meaning. It provides what a personality cannot acquire for itself, a mirror which it cannot hold before itself" (Hartmann, p. 369, 1932). Certainly love is a salient component in intimate friendship.

Others may actually know more about us than we know about ourselves. Within the context of love this can be very beneficial. Alfred Schutz describes this knowledge of the other well.

> ...each of us can experience the other's thought and acts in the vivid present whereas either can grasp his own only as a past by way of reflection. I know more of the other and he knows more of me than either of us knows of his own stream of consciousness....we experience the other's acts in their vivid performance (Schutz, p.167, 1970).

Thus a friend can act as an alter-ego helping to clarify one's own understanding.

Another benefit of a good friendship is that friends can and do encourage growth and development (Foote, p. 247, 1953). It is difficult to encourage growth without expecting too much from the other. According to Hartmann there is a precarious balance required: while seeing the ideal of the other there must be a realization and acceptance of the actual of the other. Yet this balance is possible in friendship. As Frank states "Only through loving a person can we accord him the dignity he must have and feel to realize his potentialities and enable him to accord worth and dignity to others" (Frank, p. 44, 1953).

The relationship itself is an atmosphere for advancement. It is not one person who grows in the relationship but it is both who grow together. "Love is that relationship between one person and another which is most conducive to the optimal development of both" (Foote, p. 247, 1953). There is, in addition, a satisfaction in watching the development and growth and advancement of one's friend as well as one's self.

Friendship is part of one's foundation in understanding the world. Friendship can act as a means of affirming reality. According to Albert and Brigante

> friends help to verify and objectify an individual's personal cognition of the world....friendship relationships appear to be a social validation process par excellence offering comparison of parental orientations and ideology...[and it] acts as a source of significance for many of our perceptions, opinions, attitudes, thoughts, feelings about ourselves and our world (Albert and Brigante, p. 34, 1962).

It is important to one's security to have persons with which to associate who are in harmony with one's own beliefs.

There is a sense of safety within friendship. Mutual cooperation supports those within the friendship and the endeavors undertaken together. Friendship provides a position of status, or of high esteem for friendship proclaims another's worth by labeling the other as a *significant other*.

A strong sense of shared history and common destiny with a friend is significant to a sense of security and meaning in life. According to Albert and Brigante "We need interested and reliable others, i.e. friends, in order to live plausible, meaningful and tolerable lives" (Albert and Brigante, p. 33, 1962). Friendship provides us with some meaning to an otherwise confusing, often frightening existence. It is "personal love" says Hartmann, which "gives an ultimate meaning to life...." not in its entirety but as a germ which extends toward more complete meaning (Hartmann, p. 381, 1932).

Summary

Even though greater independent and goal directed behavior exists in our world today, people are still interested in friendship because it gives them a great deal. Certainly many of the benefits that friendship produces can be obtained in no other way, neither paying a psychotherapist to listen, nor a teacher to teach, nor a service agency to

give materials or services. People need the warm affection and companionship that develops from two individuals caring for and about one another. Friendship provides a myriad of psychological benefits. It supports, broadens, and confirms. It allows greater understanding of the world and affords greater meaning to life.

Chapter 9

Friendship for Tomorrow

Friendship can be a personally rewarding and valuable relationship. It deserves greater research attention, social sanction, and appreciation.

Personal relationships in general have received increasing consideration in the last decade. According to Perlman and Fehr "the [personal relationship] literature is replete with evidence testifying to the importance of relationships in our lives" (p. 19, 1987). Several surveys have found personal relationships are of primary importance in people's lives, ahead of money, career, and religion (Duck, p. 1, 1988). Still, interest in, and attention to, are not synonymous.

As one form of personal relation, friendship has received little social sanction. Marriage has been societally sanctioned and marriage and family relations have received far greater regard with a field of study all their own. In addition, marriage and family counseling, which attempts to repair and adjust problematic family relationships, has been around for many years.

The study of personal relations, inclusive of friendship has grown considerably in the last decade, expanding in scope and depth with improved methodologies and greater interdisciplinary sharing. One of the leaders in the field, Steve Duck, has noted the significance of this interdisciplinary nature of research he calls a distinctive *field* of personal relations. The field, according to Duck, is well served by many disciplines which can accommodate for disciplinary biases (Duck, p. vi, 1988). Sociologists, psychologists, communication and family experts are the predominant disciplines exploring personal relationships today.

Friendship itself has seen a score or more books, some more, some less theoretical and research based, in the last decade, whereas the previous fifty years produced half that many. Friendship may finally be moving toward a place of significance in this country. Yet it seems there is some distance to go before it is rightly recognized for its significance. For this to occur specific heed must be given to the study of friendship as a specific relationship within the schema of personal relationships. Friendship should be fostered and nurtured through structured approaches on individual, community, and societal levels. It should be publicly exalted and enjoyed.

The gamut of relationships labelled friendship include variations in feelings, experiences, behaviors, purposes, intentions and attention which makes its study so much harder. Particularly close

personal friendships should be explored in greater depth because of their impact on individuals and society.

Friendship brings forth the numerous rewards discussed previously. Additionally, evidence indicates that friendship, along with other close personal relationships can have a positive effect on physical and psychological well-being. In a review of literature on social interaction Reis concludes that "well-being is most likely to stem from contact with affectively close or intimate partners" (p. 34, 1984).

The social ramifications of increasing and strengthening friendship ties are also quite promising. Weaving friendships, of an intimate or more casual sort, can strengthen the social fabric building communities with people pulling together and supporting each other. Presently communities seem to evidence an absence of such connection.

The definition of close friendship given earlier bears repeating. Friendship is a relationship of two people who care for one another, feel a sense of commitment and sharing and who experience the relationship as one of equality and reciprocity. The nature of friendship allows it to cross ethnic, racial, religious, and gender barriers, making it a viable relationship for personal growth and community enhancement.

Continuing Research

Cross-disciplinary research on friendship, within the context of other personal relationships needs to advance. Hinde (1981) has discussed the need for an "adequate descriptive base" encompassing close personal relationships and more formal role relationships (p. 6-7). Hinde goes on to identify important directions for future study which should cover content, depth, and interactive type. Duck (1988) points first to the positive movement found in the developing field of personal relationships and then identifies the directions for continued advancement. He cautions against future research getting caught in practices and perceptions of previous social research which have limited study. According to Duck

the best current research on relating to others is cross-disciplinary and process-oriented; it stresses the behavioural components of relating in the everyday lives of relational participants in addition to pure cognition, attitudes, or attribution; and it has a place for interpersonal communication through which many relational processes actually operate....It emphasizes the non-automatic nature of relating, its two sidedness... (p. 138, 1988).

To study relationships, behavioral, cognitive, and affective components of intra- and inter-personal must be contextually considered. According to McCarthy (1981) the "scientific study of personal relationships will never be an easy or routine undertaking; the phenomena are too complex and variable for simple theoretical notions....methodological pluralism is the only road..."(p. 23-24).

Social psychological research, a forerunner in the area of personal relations studies, focused on correlational and laboratory studies as the major means of gathering data about relationships. Future research needs to include multi-stage correlation studies, longitudinal studies and laboratory studies using relational partners, rather than strangers (McCarthy, p. 31-37, 1981). Directed longitudinal research such as record keeping or relationship journals give an added dimension. A phenomenological approach to the study of friendship as conducted by Fox et al. (1985) and Reohr (1985), allows for more relational nuances to be observed. As Olson (1977) points out in his article "Insiders' and outsiders' views of relationships," both subjective and objective realities, which don't always concur, are crucial in understanding relationships. As social context is a salient factor in relationships, cross cultural investigation is necessary as well as cross life span study.

There is a long way to go. According to Acitelli and Duck (1987), measures of intimacy are inadequate (p. 299). Measures of social exchange and reward/cost analyses are too narrow to cover the expanse of experience in personal relationships. Understanding intimacy and the broad concept of reciprocity are fundamental in understanding close relationships and need further investigation. Assessments of other components of personal relationships need to be developed or improved.

Reciprocity, as described herein, is a broader concept than social exchange and as such it can help build a descriptive base for relationships. Such research should not set out with specific measures

of reciprocity but rather employ a phenomenological approach permitting description by participants and observation by researchers who hold preconceptions in abeyance while permitting the subjects to be real participants in the research.

Support for Relationships

In addition to research on existing relationships there is a need for understanding of dissolution and repair of personal relations. (See Duck's edited volume *Personal relationships, Vol. 5: Repairing personal relationships.*) Such study can help foster new relationships and work to help repair existing ones. Active attention also is needed to helping people to develop cognitive and functional understanding of relationships thus increasing the likelihood of friendship development.

Personal

Clinicians should continue to contribute to the cross-disciplinary field of personal relationships providing directions for tested and innovative methods to facilitate development, enhancement, adjustment, and repair of personal relations.

Comparisons of psychotherapy and friendship are reasonably common from the perspective of the therapist as friend and friendship as therapeutic. Both clearly have some basis in fact. Innovative methods to assist those who don't make friends easily, that is, making loneliness therapy less necessary, would be valuable.

Specific procedures to teach social skills and organize activities for friendship enhancement for children and adults have been elaborated by several authors (for example, Stocking, Arezzo, and Leavitt, 1979 and Dawley, 1980). Jones, Hanssoon, and Cutrona (1984) identify ways of increasing interpersonal ties and discuss values of behavioral skills training as interventions with the lonely, young and old. Other more directive approaches for friendship development might be used like those identified by Gurdin (1986) using a structured group for friendship therapy.

More widespread application of these or similar methods both for children and adults in both family and community settings could net worthwhile individual and social outcomes.

There should be recognition of friendship as worthy of therapeutic intervention. Therapists clearly spend major portions of time with their clients discussing relationships and associated problems.

Specialization in friendship counseling with individual and friendship pairs, and group therapy for friendship should be a direction for the future. Friendship therapists or counselors need to understand the similarities and differences friendship has with other personal relationships. They also need to acknowledge the societal context. Procedures specific to friendship functioning could be employed with use of personal history, role playing and other means of practice.

Societal

Social approaches to friendship enhancement could include a number of possible arrangements. Systems for initiating and constructing connections which might lead to long term friendship should be developed. Our mobile society curtails opportunities for association. Lack of small, personal, religious and community centers decreases chances of meeting people in a relaxed, friendly atmosphere. Organizations with the specific purpose of friendship formation could be valuable today.

Ordering friendships within our communities, schools, and places of work would be an appropriate starting place. Although in American society friendship is seen as tied to the notion of volition, arranged friendships are not uncommon in other societies with very rewarding outcomes. Structuring work relationships would be advantageous for people new to the milieu. It would be logical since we develop friends at work most often because of some assignment or responsibility which causes paths to cross. Why not set particular paths to cross? And why not in schools? Such a practice occurs on an occasional basis. Why not structure school friends for everyone and encourage cooperative rather than competitive activities for friends?

In communities, structured friendships could function as an advanced version of the welcome wagon. Eventually such connections would foster improved communities relations and develop more supportive and interdependent communities. This might ameliorate some of the negative effects of the high mobility of this society. Large apartment complexes evidence the need for some connecting devices with moving vans a daily occurrence. Cities, towns, and country environs today seem to need community enhancement methods.

Conclusion

The last decade has seen a tremendous increase in the quality and quantity of research on personal relationships. There is much to be done with this complex topic so pervasive and important to our lived experience. Friendship, because of its incredible value and impact on our lives, should receive greater attention and sanction. The field of personal relationships will be exciting to watch over the next decade.

Bibliography

Acitelli, L.K. & Duck, S. (1987). Intimacy as the proverbial elephant. D. Perlman & S. Duck (Eds.), *Intimate relationship: Development, dynamics, and deterioration*. Newbury Park, California: Sage Publ.

Adams, J.S. (1965). Inequity in social exchange. In L. Berkowitz (Ed.). *Advances in Experimental Social Psychology* (Vol. 2). New York: Academic Press.

Albert, S. & Brigante, T.R. (1962). The psychology of friendship relations: Social factors. *Journal of Social Psychology*, 56, 33-47.

Allan, G. (1979). *Sociology of friendship and kinship*. London: George Allen & Unwin.

Allenby, A.I. (1954, July). *Relationship and healing*. Guild of Pastoral Psychology, Guild Lecture 84. Originally delivered at conference of Guild of Pastoral Psychology, Bristol.

Allport, G. (1950). Psychological approach to the study of love and hate. In P. Sorokin (Ed.), *Explorations in altruistic love and behavior*. Boston: Beacon Press.

Andreyeva, G.M. & Gozman, L.J. (1981). Interpersonal relationships and social context. In S. Duck & R. Gilmour (Eds.), *Personal relationships, Vol. 1. Studying personal relationships* (pp. 47-66). New York: Academic Press.

Argyle, M. (1983). *The psychology of interpersonal behavior* (4th ed.). Middlesex, England: Penguin Books.

Argyle, M. & Henderson, M. (1984). The rules of friendship. *Journal of Social and Personal Relationships*, 1(2), 211- 238.

Aristotle. (1962). *Nichomachen ethics*. (M. Oswald, Trans.). Indianapolis: Liberal Arts Press.

Aristotle. (1921). *The works of Aristotle*. (J. Solomon, Ed. and Trans.). London: Oxford University at Clarendon Press.

Aristotle. (1932). *The rhetoric of Aristotle*. (L. Cooper, Trans.). New York: Appleton-Century-Crofts.

Aronson, E. (1960). *The social animal* (2nd ed.). San Francisco: W.H. Freeman.

Bacon, F. (1966). *Francis Bacon's essays* (rev. ed.). London: Everyman's Library.

Becker, H. (1956). *Man in reciprocity*. New York: Fredrick A. Praeger.

Becker, H. & Useem, R.H. (1942). Sociological analysis of the dyad. *American Sociological Review, 7*, 14-21.

Beier, E.G., Rossi, A.M. & Garfield, R.L. (1961). Similarity plus dissimilarity of personality: Basis for friendship. *Psychological Reports, 8*, 3-8.

Bell, R.R. (1981a). *Worlds of friendship*. Beverly Hills: Sage Publications.

Bell, R.R. (1981b). Friendships of women and men. *Psychology of Women Quarterly, 5*, 402-417.

Bellak, L. (1963). Personality structure in a changing world. In P. Olson (Ed.), *America as a mass society* (pp. 415-8). London: Collier-Macmillan.

Bender, H. (1974). *The philosophy of Martin Buber*. New York: Monarch Press.

Bensman, J. & Lilienfeld, R. (1979, October). Friendship and alienation. *Psychology Today*.

Berger, P.L. (1977). *Facing up to modernity*. New York: Basic Books.

Berger, P.L. & Luckman, T. (1967). *The social construction of reality*. New York: Anchor Books.

Bernard, J. (1982). *The future of marriage* (2nd ed.). New Haven: Yale University Press.

Berscheid, E. & Walster, E.H. (1969). *Interpersonal attraction*. Reading, Massachusetts: Addison-Wesley.

Berscheid, E. & Walster, E. (1974). A little bit about love. In T.L. Houston (Ed.), *Foundations of interpersonal attraction* (pp. 355-381). New York: Academic Press.

Black, H.C. (1979). *Black's law dictionary* (5th ed.). St. Paul, Minnesota: West Publ. Co.

Black, P.A. (1898). *Friendship*. Chicago: Fleming H. Revell.

Blau, P.M. (1969). Exchange of social rewards. In L.A. Coser & B. Rosenberg (Eds.), *Sociological Theory* (3rd ed.) (pp. 93-6). London: Macmillan.

Block, J.D. (1980). *Friendship: How to give it and how to get it*. New York: Collier Books.

Blom J. (1969). *Some impressions and hypotheses concerning the source, quality, and revelance of friendship*. Unpublished manuscript, University of Bergen.

Bolton, C. (1961). Mate selection as the development of a relationship. *Marriage and Family Living, 23*, 234-40.

Booth, A. (1972). Sex and social participation. *American Sociological Review, 37*, 183-193.

Bowles, S. & Gintus, H. (1976). *Schooling in capitalist America*. New York: Basic Books.

Brain, R. (1976). *Friends and lovers*. New York: Basic Books.

Brenton, M. (1974). *Friendship*. New York: Stein & Day.

Bronfenbrenner, U. (1970). *Two worlds of childhood: U.S. and U.S.S.R.* New York: Pocket Books.

Bronfenbrenner, U. (1977, May). Nobody home: The erosion of the American family. *Psychology Today*.

Bry, A. (1979). *Friendship: How to have a friend and be a friend.* New York: Grosset and Dunlap.

Buber, M. (1957). *Pointing the way: Collected essays.* M. Friedman (Ed. & Trans.). London: Routledge & Kegan Paul.

Buber, M. (1965a). *Between man and man.* R.G. Smith (Trans.). New York: Macmillan.

Buber, M. (1965b). *The knowledge of man.* M. Friedman (Ed.). M. Friedman & R.G. Smith (Trans.). New York: Harper Torchbooks.

Buber, M. (1966). *The way of response.* N.N. Glatzer (Ed.). New York: Schocken Books.

Buber, M. (1967). *A believing humanism: Gleanings by Martin Buber.* R.N. Anshen (Ed.), M. Friedman (Trans.). New York: Simon & Schuster.

Buber, M. (1970). *I and thou.* W. Kaufmann (Trans.). New York: Charles Scribner's Sons.

Burgess, R.L. (1981). Relationships in marriage and the family. In S. Duck & R. Gilmour (Eds.), *Personal relationship: Vol. 1. Studying personal relationships* (pp. 179-196). New York: Academic Press.

Burnaby, J. (1938). *Amor dei: A study of the religion of St. Augustine.* London: Hodder & Stoughton.

Buscaglia, L.F. (1972). *Love.* Thorofare, New Jersey: Charles B. Slack.

Cabot, R.C. (1914). *What men live by work, play, love, worship.* Boston: Houghton Mifflin.

Candy, S.G., Troll, L.E. & Levy, S.G. (1981). A developmental exploration of friendship functions in women. *Psychology of Women Quarterly,* 5, 456-472.

Carpenter, E. (Ed.). (1902). *Iolaus: An anthology of friendship.* London: Swan Sonnenschein.

Cicero, M.T. (1967). *On old age and on friendship.* H.G. Edinger (Trans.). Indianapolis: Library of Liberal Arts.

Clark, M.S. (1981). Non-comparability of benefits given and received: A cue to the existence of friendship. *Social Psychology Quarterly,* 44, 375-81.

Clark, M.S. (1985). Implications of relationship type for understanding compatibility. In W. Ickes (Ed.), *Compatible and incompatible relationships.* New York: Springer-Verlag.

Clark, M.S. & Mills, J. (1979). Interpersonal attraction in exchange and communal relationships. *Journal of Personal and Social Psychology.* 37 (1), 12-24.

Cobb, S. (1976). Social support as a moderator of life stress. *Psychosomatic Medicine,* 38, 300-314.

Coehlo, G. (1959). A guide to literature on friendship: A selectively annotated bibliography. *Psychological Newsletter,* 10, 365-394.

Cohen, Y.A. (1961). Patterns of friendship. In Y.A. Cohen (Ed.), *Social structure and personality: A casebook.* New York: Holt, Rinehart & Winston.

Combs, A.W., Avila, D.L. & Purkey, W.W. (1971). *Helping relationships: Basic concepts for the helping professions.* Boston: Allyn & Bacon.

Conde, B. (1916). *The business of being a friend.* Boston: Houghton Mifflin.

Cooley, C.H. (1956). *Human nature and the social order* (rev. ed.). Glencoe, Illinois: Free Press.

Coser, L.A. & Rosenberg, B. (Eds.). (1969). *Sociological theory* (3rd ed.). London: Macmillan.

Cotroneo, M. (n.d.). *A parenting paradigm for colleague relationships.* Unpublished manuscript, Department of Family Psychiatry, Eastern Pennsylvania Psychiatry Institute.

Cotroneo, M. & Krasner, B. (1977). *Two paradigms for balance in relationships.* Unpublished manuscript.

Cowburn, J. (1967). *Love and the person.* London: Geoffrey Chapman.

D'Arcy, M.C. (1947). *The mind and heart of love.* New York: Henry Holt.

Davidson, S. & Packard, T. (1981). The therapeutic value of friendship between women. *Psychology of Women Quarterly,* 5 495-510.

Davis, M. (1973). *Intimate relations.* New York: Free Press.

Dawley, H.H. (1980). *Friendship: How to make and keep friends.* Englewood Cliffs, New Jersey: Prentice Hall.

Denzin, N.K. (1970). Rules of conduct and the study of deviant behavior. In G.J. McCall, M.J. McCall, N.K. Denzin, G.D. Suttles, & S.D.Kurth, *Social relationships.* Chicago: Aldine Publ.

DePaoli, D.A. (1971). *Freedom and mutuality.* (Doctoral dissertation, Fordham University, 1971).

Deutsch, M. (1979). A critical review of "Equity Theory": An alternative perspective on the social psychology of justice. *International Journal of Group Tensions* (pp. 20-49).

deVries, E. (1968). Explorations in reciprocity. In E. deVries (Ed.), *Essays on reciprocity* (pp. 9-19). Netherlands: Mouton.

Dewey, J. (1958). *Experience and nature.* New York: Dover Publ.

Dewey, J. (1960). *On experience, nature, and freedom.* R.J. Berstein (Ed.). New York: Bobbs-Merrill.

Diamond, M.L. (1967). Dialogue and theology. In P.A. Schilpp & M. Friedman (Eds.), *The philosophy of Martin Buber* (pp. 235-247). LaSalle, Illinois: Open Court.

Dickens, W.J. & Perlman, D. (1981). Friendship over the life-cycle. In S. Duck & R. Gilmour (Eds.), *Personal relationships: Vol. 2. Developing personal relationships* (pp. 91-122). New York: Academic Press.

DuBois, C. (Ed.). (1955). *Studies of friendship*. Unpublished manuscript, Harvard University Dept. of Social Relations, Peabody Museum Library.

DuBois, C. (1974). The gratuitous act. In E. Leyton (Ed.), *The compact: Selected dimensions of friendship* (pp. 15-26). Newfoundland Social and Economic Paper 3. Institute of Social and Economic Research, Memorial University of Newfoundland. Toronto: University of Toronto Press.

Duck, S. (1982). A topography of relationship disengagement and dissolution. In S. Duck (Ed.), *Personal relationships: Vol. 4. Dissolving personal relationships* (pp. 1-30). New York: Academic Press.

Duck, S. (1983). *Friends for life: The psychology of close relationships*. New York: St. Martin's Press

Duck, S. (1984). A perspective on the repair of personal relationships: Repair of what, when? In S. Duck (Ed.), *Personal relationships: Vol. 5. Repairing personal relationship* (pp. 163-184). New York: Academic Press.

Duck, S. (1986). *Human relationships: An introduction to social psychology*. Beverly Hills: Sage Publications.

Duck, S. (1988). *Relating to others*. Chicago: Dorsey Press.

Duck, S., Lock, A., McCall, G., Fitzpatrick, M.A. & Coyne, J.C. (1984). Social and personal relationships: a joint editorial. *Journal of Social and Personal Relationships*, 1(1), 1-10.

Duck, S. & Miell, D. (1985). Towards a comprehension of friendship development and breakdown. In H. Tajfel, C. Fraser & J. Jaspers (Eds.), *Social dimensions: European developments in social psychology* (vol. 1). Cambridge: Cambridge University Press.

Duck, S. & Sants, H. (1983). On the origin of the specious: Are personal relationships really interpersonal states? *Journal of Social and Clinical Psychology*, 1(1), 27-41.

Durkheim, E. (1933). *The division of labor in society*. G. Simpson (Trans.). New York: Free Press.

Ekeh, P.P. (1974). *Social exchange theory: The two traditions*. Cambridge: Harvard University Press.

Emerson, R.W. (1969). *Essays and essays: Second series*. Columbus, Ohio: Charles E. Merrill.

Erikson, E.H. (1963). *Childhood and society* (2 ed.). New York: W.W. Norton.

Farber, L. (1966). *The ways of the will*. New York: Basic Books.

Festinger, L., Schachter, S. & Back, K. (1967). *Social pressures in informal groups*. California: Stanford University Press.

Firth, R. (1936). Bond friendship in Tikopia. In L.H. Dudley-Buxton (Ed.), *Custom is king*. Plymouth, England: Mayflower Press.

Firth, R. (1967). *Tikopia ritual and belief*. Boston: Beacon Press.

Fischer, J.L. & Narus, L.R. (1981). Sex roles and intimacy in same sex and other sex relationships. *Psychology of Women Quarterly*, 5, 444-455.

Flemming, E.G. (1932). Best friends. *Journal of Social Psychology*, 3, 385-390.

Foa, E.B. & Foa, U.G. (1980). Resource theory: Interpersonal behavior as exchange. In K.J. Gergen, M.S. Greenberg, & R.H. Willis (Eds.), *Social exchange: Advances in theory and research*. New York: Plenum Press.

Foote, N.N. (1953). Love. *Psychiatry*, 16(3), 245-251.

Fortier, T.L. (1970). *On friendship: Its nature, kinds, and effects in human life*. (Doctoral dissertation, De L'Universite Laval, 1970).

Fox, M., Gibbs, M. & Auerbach, D. (1985). Age and gender dimensions of friendship. *Psychology of Women Quarterly*, 9, 489-502.

Frank, L. (1953). On loving. In *The meaning of love* (pp. 25-44). New York: Julian Press.

Friedman, M. (1975). Healing through meeting: A dialogical approach to psychotherapy. *American Journal of Psychoanalysis*, Part 1, 35(3), 255-267; Part 2, 35(4), 343-354.

Fromm, E. (1956). *The art of loving*. R.N Anshen (Ed.). New York: Harper & Brothers.

Fromm, E. (1960). *Escape from freedom*. New York: Rinehart & Winston.

Furman, W. (1984). Enhancing children's peer relations and friendships. In S. Duck (Ed.), *Personal relationships: Vol. 5, Repairing personal relationships* (pp. 101-125). New York: Academic Press.

Gadlin, H. (1977). Private lives and public order: A critical view of the history of intimate relations in the United States. In G. Levinger & H.L. Raush (Eds.), *Close relationships* (pp. 33-72). Amherst, Massachusetts: University of Massachusetts Press.

Galbraith, J.K. (1958). *The affluent society* (rev. ed.). New York: Mentor Books.

Gasset, O.Y. (1957). *On love*. T. Tablot (Trans.). New York: Meridan Books.

Gergen, K. (1969). *The psychology of behavior exchange*. Reading, Massachusetts: Addison-Wesley.

Gilligan, C. (1982). *In a different voice*. Cambridge, Massachusetts: Harvard University Press.

Gillis, J. (1976). *Friends: The power and potential of the company you keep.* New York: Coward, McCann and Geoghegan.

Goodman, G. (1972). *Companionship therapy.* San Francisco: Jossey-Bass.

Gottlieb, B.H. (1985). Social support and the study of personal relationships. *Journal of Social and Personal Relationships,* 2(3), 351-375.

Gould, C. (1977). *Beyond causality in the social sciences: Reciprocity as a model of non-exploitative social relations.* Unpublished manuscript. Originally presented, Boston Colloquium for the Philosophy of Science, Boston University.

Gouldner, A.W. (1960). The norm of reciprocity: A preliminary statement. *American Sociological Review,* 25(2), 161-178.

Gouldner, A.W. (1970). *The coming crisis of western sociology.* New York: Basic Books.

Gouldner, A.W. (1973). *For sociology: Renewal and critique in sociology today.* New York: Basic Books.

Greeley, A. (1971). *The friendship game.* New York: Image Books.

Greenberg, J. (1983). Equity and equality as clues to the relationship between exchange participants. *European Journal of Social Psychology,* 13, 195-196.

Greer, S. (1963). Individual participation in mass society. In P. Olson (Ed.), *America in a mass society* (pp. 327-336). London: Collier-Macmillan.

Guitton, J. (1966). *Human love.* Chicago: Franciscan Herald Press.

Gurdin, J.B. (1978). *Amitie/friendship: The socio-cultural construction of friendship in contemporary Montreal.* (Doctoral dissertation, Universite de Montreal, 1978).

Gurdin, J. (1986). The therapy of friendship. *Small Group Behavior* 17 (4), 444-457.

Halverson, C.F. & Shore, R.E. (1969). Self-disclosure and interpersonal functioning. *Journal of Consulting and Clinical Psychology*, 33(2), 213-217.

Hampton-Turner, C. (1970). *Radical man: The process of psycho-social development*. Cambridge, Massachusetts: Schenkman Publ.

Harlow, H.F. (1958). The nature of love. *American Psychologist*, 13, 673-685.

Harlow, H.F. (1971). *Learning to love*. New York: Ballantine Books.

Harper, R. (1966). *Human love: Existential and mystical*. Baltimore: Johns Hopkins Press.

Hartmann, N. (1932). *Moral values: Vol. 2 Ethics* (3 Vols.). S. Coit (Trans.). New York: Macmillan.

Hartup, W.W. (1975). The origins of friendships. In M. Lewis & L.A. Rosenblum (Eds.), *Friendship and peer relationships*. New York: John Wiley & Sons.

Hatfield, E., Traupmann, J., Sprecher, S., Utne, M., & Hay, J. (1985). Equity and intimate relations: Recent research. In W. Ickes (Ed.). *Compatible and incompatible relationships*. New York: Springer-Verlag.

Hays, R.B. (1984). The development and maintenance of friendship. *Journal of Social and Personal Relationships*, 1(1), 75-98.

Hays, R.B. (1989). The day-to-day functioning of close versus casual friendships. *Journal of Social and Personal Relationships*, 6(1), 21-37.

Hazo, R. (1967). *The idea of love*. New York: Frederick A. Praeger.

Hess, B. (1972). Friendship. In M.W. Riley, M. Johnson & A. Foner (Eds.), *Aging and society* (Vol. 3) (pp. 357-393). New York: Russell Sage Foundation.

Hinde, R.A. (1979). *Toward understanding relationships.* New York: Academic Press.

Hinde, R.A. (1981). The bases of a science of interpersonal relationships. In S. Duck & R. Gilmour (Eds.), *Personal relationships: Vol. 1. Studying personal relationships* (pp. 1-22). New York: Academic Press.

Hofstadter, R. (1955). *Social Darwinism in American thought* (rev. ed.). Boston: Beacon Press.

Holt, R.W. (1982). Perceptions of the equity and exchange processes in dyadic social relationships. *Perceptual and Motor Skills,* 54, 303-320.

Homans, G.C. (1961). *Social behavior: Its elementary forms.* New York: Harcourt, Brace & World.

Hunt, M. (1963). The age of love. In P. Olson (Ed.), *America as a mass society* (pp. 539-547). London: Collier-Macmillan.

Huston, T.L. & Burgess, R.D. (Eds.). (1979). *Social exchange in developing relationships.* New York: Academic Press.

Hutter, H. (1978). *Politics as friendship.* Waterloo, Canada: Wilfrid Laurier University Press.

Illich, I. (1971). *Deschooling society.* New York: Harrow Books.

James, M. & Savary, L.M. (1976). *The heart of friendship.* New York: Harper & Row.

Johann, R.O. (1966). *The meaning of love.* Glen Rock, New Jersey: Deus Books, Paulist Press.

Johann, R.O. (1968). *Building the human.* New York: Herder & Herder.

Johnson, A. (1953). Love of friends. In A. Montagu (Ed.), *The meaning of love.* New York: Julian Press.

Johnson, F.L. & Aries, E.J. (1983). The talk of women friends. *Women's Studies International Forum,* 6(4), pp. 353-361.

Jones, W.H., Hansson, R.D., & Cutrona, C. (1984). Helping the lonely: Issues of intervention with young and older adults. In S. Duck (Ed.), *Personal relationships: Vol. 5, Repairing personal relationships.* New York: Academic Press.

Jourard, S. (1959). Self disclosure and other cathexis. *Journal of Abnormal and Social Psychology,* 59, 428-431.

Jourard, S. (1971). *The transparent self.* New York: D. Van Nostrand.

Jourard, S. (1974). *The healthy personality.* New York: Macmillan Publ.

Jourard, S. & Lasakow, P. (1958). Some factors in self-disclosure. *Journal of of Abnormal and Social Psychology,* 56, 91-98.

Kant, I. (1963). *Lectures on ethics.* L. Infield (Trans.). New York: Harper Torchbooks.

Keith-Lucas, A. (1972). *Giving and taking help.* Chapel Hill, North Carolina: University of North Carolina Press.

Kelley, H.H., Berscheid, E., Christensen, A., Harvey, J.H., Huston, T.L., Levinger, G., McClintock, E., Peplau, L.A. & Peterson, D.R. (1983). *Close relationships.* New York: W.H. Freeman.

Kierkegaard, S. (1962). *The present age.* A. Dru (Trans.). New York: Harper Torchbooks.

Kilpatrick, W. (1975). *Identity and intimacy.* New York: Dell Publ.

Knight, F.H. (1947). *Freedom and reform: Essays in economics and social philosophy.* New York: Harper & Brothers.

Kohlberg, L. (1969). Stage and sequences: The cognitive-development approach to socialization. In D.A. Goslin (Ed.), *Handbook of socialization theory and research.* Chicago: Rand McNally.

Krasner, B.R. (1977, March). *Beyond manipulation: Reciprocity in family and community relations.* Paper presented at Family Counselling Workshop, LaSalle College.

Kurth, S.B. (1970). Friendships and friendly relations. In G.J. McCall, M.J. McCall, N.K. Denzin, G.D. Suttles, & S.B. Kurth, *Social relationships*. Chicago: Aldine Publ.

LaGaipa, J.J. (1981). A systems approach to personal relationships. In S. Duck & R. Gilmour (Eds.), *Personal relationships: Vol. 1. Studying personal relationships* (pp. 67-90). New York: Academic Press.

Lasch, C. (1976, September). The narcissistic society. *The New York Review*, 23(15), 5-13.

Lazarsfeld, P.F. & Merton, R.K. (1954). Friendship as social process: A substantive and methodological analysis. In M. Berger, T. Abel, & C.H. Page (Eds.), *Freedom and control in modern society* (pp. 18-66). New York: D. Van Nostrand.

Lee, J.A. (1977). A typology of styles of loving. *Personality and Social Psychology Bulletin*, 3, 173-182.

Leefeldt, C. & Callenback, E. (1979). *The art of friendship*. New York: Pantheon.

Lepp, I. (1966). *The ways of friendship*. B. Murchland (Trans.). New York: Macmillan Publ.

Levinas, E. (1967). Martin Buber and the theory of knowledge. In P. Schilpp & M. Friedman (Eds.), *The philosophy of Martin Buber*. LaSalle, Illinois: Open Court.

Levinger, G. (1977). The embrace of lives: Changing and unchanging. In G. Levinger & H.L. Raush (Eds.), *Close relationships*. Amherst, Massachusetts: University of Massachusetts.

Levi-Strauss, C. (1969a). *The elementary structures of kinship*. J.R. von Sturmer & R. Needham (Eds.), J.H. Bell (Trans.). Boston: Beacon Press.

Levi-Strauss, C. (1969b). The principle of reciprocity. In L.A. Coser & B. Rosenberg (Eds.), *Sociological Theory* (3rd ed.), (pp. 77-86). London: Macmillan.

Lewis, C.S. (1960). *The four loves.* New York: Harcourt Brace Jovanovich.

Lewis, M. & Rosenblum, L.A. (Eds.). (1975). *Friendship and peer relationships.* New York: John Wiley & Sons.

Leyton, E. (Ed.). (1974). *The compact: Selected dimensions of friendship.* Newfoundland Social and Economic Paper 3. Institute of Social and Economic Research, Memorial University of Newfoundland. Toronto: University of Toronto Press.

Lloyd, S., Cate, R. & Henton, J. (1982). Equity and rewards as predictors of the satisfaction in casual and intimate relationships. *The Journal of Psychology*, 110, 43-48.

Locke, H.J. (1968). *Predicting adjustment in marriage.* New York: Greenwood Press.

Lowenthal, M.F., Thurnher, M. & Chiriboga, D. (1977). Life-course perspectives on friendship. *Four stages of life* (pp. 48-61). San Francisco: Jossey-Bass.

Luft, J. (1969). *Of human interaction.* Palo Alto, California: National Press Books.

Lund, M. (1981). The development of investment and commitment scales for predicting continuity in personal relationships. *Journal of Social and Personal Relationships*, 2(1), 3-23.

Lynch, J.J. (1977). *The broken heart: The medical consequences of loneliness.* New York: Basic Books.

MacBeath, A. (1952). *Experiments in living.* London: Macmillan.

MacMurray, J. (1957). *Self as agent.* London: Farber & Farber.

MacMurray, J. (1961). *Persons in relation.* London: Farber & Farber.

Maier, N.R. (1973). *Psychology in industrial organizations* (4th ed.). Boston: Houghton Mifflin.

Malinowski, B. (1961). *Argonauts of the western Pacific.* New York: E.P. Dutton. (Original work published in 1922).

Malinowski, B. (1969). The principle of give and take, and Reciprocity as the basis of social cohesion. In L.A. Coser & B. Rosenberg (Eds.), *Sociological Theory* (pp. 73-6; 204-5). London: Macmillan.

Mandelbaum, D.G. (1936). Friendship in North America. *Man,* 36, 205-6.

Mangam, I.L. (1981). Relationships at work: Tension and tolerance. In S. Duck & R. Gilmour (Eds.), *Personal relationships: Vol 1, Studying personal relationships* (pp. 197-214). New York: Academic Press.

Marty, M.E. (1980). *Friendship.* Allen, Texas: Argus Communications.

Maslow, A. (1953). Love in healthy people. In A. Montagu (Ed.), *The meaning of love.* New York: Julian Press.

Maslow, A. (1968). *Toward a psychology of being* (2nd ed.). New York: D. Van Nostrand.

Maslow, A. (1971). *The farther reaches of human nature.* S. Miller (Ed.). New York: Viking Press.

Mauss, M. (1967). *The gift.* I. Cunnison (Trans.). New York: W.W. Norton.

May, R. (1969). *Love and will.* New York: W.W. Norton.

Mayeroff, M. (1971). *On caring.* New York: Harper & Row.

Mayo, C. & LaFrance, M. (1977). *Evaluating research in social psychology.* Monterey, California: Brooks/Cole.

McCall, G.J. (1970). The social organization of relationships. In McCall, G.J., McCall, M.J., Denzin, N.K., Suttles, G.D. & Kurth, S.B., *Social relationships.* Chicago: Aldine Publ.

McCall, M.J. (1970). Boundary rules in relationships and encounters. In McCall, G.J., McCall, M.J., Denzin, N.K., Suttles, G.D., & Kurth, S.B., *Social relationships*. Chicago: Aldine Publ.

McCarthy, B. (1981). Studying personal relationships. In S. Duck & R. Gilmour (Eds.), *Personal relationships: Vol. 1. Studying personal relationships* (pp. 23-46). New York: Academic Press.

Mead, G.H. (1934). *Mind, self, and society*. Chicago: University of Chicago Press.

Mehlman, B. (1962). Similarity in friendships. *Journal of Social Psychology*, 57, 195-202.

Melbin, M. (1972). *Alone and with others: A grammar of interpersonal behavior*. New York: Harper & Row.

Menninger, K. (1942). *Love against hate*. New York: Harcourt, Brace, & Co.

Menninger, K., Mayman, M. & Pruyser, P. (1963). *The vital balance*. New York: Viking Press.

Merrens, M.R. & Garrett, J.B. (1978). The Protestant ethic scale as a predictor of repetitive work performance. In D.W. Organ (Ed.), *The applied psychology of work behavior*. Dallas, Texas: Business Publ.

Michaels, J.W., Acock, A.C. & Edwards, J.N. (1986). Social exchange and equity determinants of relationship commitment. *Journal of Social and Personal Relationships*, 3, 161-175.

Millet, J. (1951). Friend-friend. In M.M. Hughes (Ed.), *The people in your life*. New York: Alfred A. Knopf.

Mitchell, W.A. (1966). Amicatherapy: Theoretical perspectives and an example of practice. *Community Mental Health Journal*, 2(4), 307-314.

Montagu, A. (1950). The origin and nature of social life and the biological basis of cooperation. In P. Sorokin (Ed.), *Explorations in altruistic love and behavior* (pp. 76-91). Boston: Beacon Press.

Montagu, A. (1951). *On being human.* New York: Henry Schuman.

Montagu, A. (1953a). *The direction of human development* (rev. ed.). New York: Hawthorn Books.

Montagu, A. (Ed.). (1953b). *The meaning of love.* New York: The Julian Press.

Montaigne (1949). Of friendship. In *Selected essays* (rev. ed.), (pp. 59-73). (C. Cotton & W. Hazlitt, Trans.). New York: Random House.

Morgan, W. R. & Sawyer, J. (1967). Bargaining, expectations, and the preference for equality over equity. *Journal of Personality and Social Psychology,* 6(2), 139-149.

Morgan, W. R. & Sawyer, J. (1979). Equality, equity, and procedural justice in social exchange. *Social Psychology Quarterly.* 42(1), 71-75.

Morton, T.L. & Douglas, M.A. (1981). Growth of relationships. In S. Duck & R. Gilmour (Eds.), *Personal relationships: Vol. 2. Developing personal relationships* (pp. 3-26). New York: Academic Press.

Murstein, B.I. & Spitz, L. (1973-4). Aristotle and friendship: A factor-analytic study. *Interpersonal Development,* 4, 21-34.

Murstein, B.I., Cerreto, M. & MacDonald, M.G. (1977). A theory and investigation of the effect of exchange-orientation on marriage and friendship. *Journal of Marriage and the Family,* 39(3), 543-548.

Naegele, K. (1958). Friendship and acquaintances: An exploration of social distinctions. *Harvard Educational Review,* 28(3), 232-252.

Nash, P. (1973). Toward a radical view of authority relationships in education. In *Educational reconstruction: Promise and challenge.* Columbus, Ohio: Charles E. Merrill.

Natanson, M. (1973). *Edmund Husserl: Philosopher of infinite tasks.* Evanston: Northwestern University Press.

Nisbet, R.A. (1962). *Community and power* (rev. ed.). New York: Oxford University Press.

O'Connell, L. (1984). An exploration of exchange in three social relationships: Kinship, friendship, and the marketplace. *Journal of Social and Personal Relationships*, 1(3), pp. 333-345.

Oliver, D.W. (1976). *Education and community*. Berkeley, California: McCutchan Publ.

Olson, D.H. (1977). Insiders' and outsiders' views of relationships: Research studies. In G. Levinger & H.L. Raush (Eds.) *Close relationships: Perspectives on the meaning of intimacy*. Amherst, Massachusetts: University of Massachusetts Press.

Olson, P. (Ed.). (1963). *America as a mass society*. London: Collier-Macmillan.

Oraison, M. (1970). Becoming oneself through others. *The Sign*, 49, 20-33.

Outka, G. (1972). *Agape*. New Haven: Yale University Press.

Ouchi, W.G. (1981). *Theory z*. Reading, Massachusetts: Addison-Wesley Publ.

Palisi, B.J. & Ransford, H.E. (1987). Friendship as a voluntary relationship: Evidence from national surveys. *Journal of Social and Personal Relationships*, 4(3), 243-259.

Paine, R. (1974). Anthropological approaches to friendship. In E. Leyton (Ed.), *The compact: Selected dimensions of friendship*. Newfoundland Social and Economic Paper 3. Institute of Social and Economic Research, Memorial University of Newfoundland. Toronto: University of Toronto Press.

Panyard, C.M. (1973). Self-disclosure between friends: A validity study. *Journal of Counselling Psychology*, 20(1), 66-68.

Parsons, E.C. (1915). Friendship: A social category. *American Journal of Sociology*, 21, 230-233.

Parsons, T. & Shils, E.A. (1969). The basic structure of the interactive relationship. In L.A. Coser & B. Rosenberg (Eds.), *Sociological theory* (3rd ed.) (pp. 87-9). London: Macmillan.

Peters, R. (1974). Personal understanding and personal relationships. In T. Mischel (Ed.), *Understanding other persons*. Totowa, New Jersey: Rowman Littlefield.

Phillips, G.M. & Metzger, N.J. (1976). *Intimate communications.* Boston: Allyn & Bacon.

Piaget, J. (1965). *The moral judgement of the child.* M. Gabain (Trans.). New York: Free Press.

Pieper, J. (1974). *About love.* R. & C. Winston (Trans.). Chicago: Franciscan Herald Press.

Pitt-Rivers, J.A. (1954). *The people of the Sierra* (2nd ed.). Chicago: University of Chicago Press.

Plato (1951). *The symposium.* W. Hamilton (Trans.). New York: Penguin Books.

Pryor, F.L. & Graburn, N.H.H. (1980). The myth of reciprocity. In K.J. Gergen, M.S. Greenberg, & R.H. Willis (Eds.), *Social exchange: Advances in theories and research.* New York: Plenum.

Rake, J.M. (1970). Friendship: A fundamental description of its subjective dimension. *Humanitas,* 6(2), 161-176.

Ramey, J. (1976). *Intimate friendship.* Englewood Cliffs, New Jersey: Prentice Hall.

Ramsoy, O. (1968). Friendship. In D.L. Sills (Ed.), *International encyclopedia of the social sciences* (Vol. 6). New York: Macmillan.

Rangell, L. (1963). On friendship. *Journal of the American Psychoanalytic Association,* 11(1), 3-54.

Reis, H.T. (1984). Social interaction and well-being. In S. Duck (Ed.), *Personal relationships: Vol. 5. Repairing personal relationships* (pp. 21-46). New York: Academic Press.

Reisman, J.M. (1979). *Anatomy of friendship.* New York: Irvington Press.

Reisman, J.M. (1981). Adult friendships. In S. Duck & R. Gilmour (Eds.), *Personal relationships: Vol. 2. Developing personal relationships* (pp. 205-230). New York: Academic Press.

Reisman, J.M. & Yamokoski, T. (1974). Psychotherapy and friendship: An analysis of the communications of friends. *Journal of Counselling Psychology,* 21(4), 269-273.

Reohr, J.R. (1978). *The place of reciprocity in friendship.* Doctoral dissertation, Boston University.

Reohr, J.R. (1982, April 25). A man's best friend is friendship. *Albany Times Union.*

Reohr, J.R. (1984, February). Friendship: An important part of education. *The Clearing House* (pp. 209-12).

Reohr, J.R. (1985). Women's descriptions of their close friendships. Paper presentation, Association for Women in Psychology, New York, March.

Rogers, C. (1961). *On becoming a person.* Boston: Houghton Mifflin.

Rogers, C. (1969). *Freedom to learn.* Columbus, Ohio: Charles E. Merrill.

Rose, S.M. (1984). How friendships end: Patterns among young adults. *Journal of Social and Personal Relationships,* 1(3), 267-277.

Rose, S.M. & Roades, L. (1987). Feminism and women's friendships. *Psychology of Women Quarterly,* 11, 243-254.

Ross, R. (1970). *Obligation.* Ann Arbor, Michigan: University of Michigan Press.

Rubel, A.J. & Kupferer, H.J. (1968). Perspectives on the atomistic-type society. *Human Organization,* 27, 189-90.

Rubin, Z. (1973). *Liking and loving: An invitation to social psychology.* New York: Holt, Rinehart & Winston.

Rubin, Z. (1975). Disclosing oneself to a stranger: Reciprocity and its limits. *Journal of Experimental Social Psychology,* 11, 233-260.

Rubin, Z. (1980). *Children's friendships.* Cambridge, Massachusetts: Harvard University Press.

Sadler, W.J. (1969). *Existence and love.* New York: Charles Scribner's Sons.

Sadler, W.J. (1970). The experience of friendship. *Humanitas,* 6(2), 177-209.

Safilios-Rothschild, C. (1981). Toward a social psychology of relationships. *Psychology of Women Quarterly,* 3, 377-384.

Sapadin, L.A. (1988). Friendship and gender: Perspectives of professional men and women. *Journal of Social and Personal Relationships,* 5(4), 387-403.

Savicki, V. (1972). Outcomes of non-reciprocal self-disclosure strategies. *Journal of Personality and Social Psychology,* 23(2), 271-6.

Scheler, M. (1954). *The nature of sympathy.* P. Heath (Trans.). London: Routledge & Kegan Paul.

Schilpp, P.A. & Friedman, M. (Eds.). (1967). *The philosophy of Martin Buber.* LaSalle, Illinois: Open Court.

Schofield, W. (1964). *Psychotherapy: The purchase of friendship.* Englewood Cliffs, New Jersey: Prentice-Hall.

Schofield, W. (1970). The psychotherapist as friend. *Humanitas,* 6(2), 211-223.

Schutz, A. (1970). *On phenomenology and social relations.* Chicago: The University of Chicago Press.

Schutz, A. (1973). *Collected papers I: The problems of social reality.* M. Natanson (Ed.). The Hague, Netherlands: Martinue Nijhoff.

Shea, L., Thompson, L. & Blieszner, R. (1988). Resources in older adults' old and new friendships. *Journal of Social and Personal Relationships,* 5(1), 83-96.

Simmel, Georg. (1964). *The sociology of Georg Simmel* (rev. ed.). K. Wolff (Ed. & Trans.). New York: Free Press.

Singer, M.G. (1963). The golden rule. *Philosophy: The Journal of the Royal Institute of Philosophy,* 38(146), 293-314.

Slater, P.E. (1970). *The pursuit of loneliness.* Boston: Beacon Press.

Sorokin, P. (1950). Love: Its aspects, production, transformation, and accumulation. In P. Sorokin (Ed.), *Explorations of altruistic love and behavior* (4-18). Boston: Beacon Press.

Sorokin, P. (1954). *The ways and power of love.* Boston: Beacon Press.

Spiegelberg, H. (1965). *The phenomenological movement* (2nd ed.). The Hague, Netherlands: Martinus Nijhoff.

Spitz, R.A. (1946). Anaclitic depression. *Psychoanalytic Study of Children,* 1, 313-342.

Stanford, G. & Roark, A.E. (1974). *Human interaction in education.* Boston: Allyn and Bacon.

Stocking, S.H. Arezzo, D. & Leavitt, S. (1979). *Helping kids make friends.* Allen, Texas: Argus Communication.

Sullivan, H.S. (1953). *The interpersonal theory of psychiatry.* New York: W.W. Norton.

Suttles, G.D. (1970). Friendship as a social institution. In G.J. McCall, M.J. McCall, N.K. Denzin, G.D. Suttles, & S.B. Kurth, *Social relationships.* Chicago: Aldine Publ.

Thibaut, J.W. & Kelley, H.H. (1959). *The social psychology of groups.* New York: John Wiley.

Thompson, W.R. & Nishimura, R. (1952). Some determinants of friendship. *Journal of Personality,* 20(3), 305-314.

Thoreau, H.D. (1960). *Walden and civil disobedience* (rev. ed.). New York: Signet Classics.

Tillich, P. (1957). *Dynamics of faith.* New York: Harper & Row.

Toffler, A. (1972). *Future shock.* New York: Bantam Books.

Tornblom, K.Y. & Fredholm, E.M. (1984). Attribution of friendship: The influence of the nature and comparability of resources given and received. *Social Psychology Quarterly,* 47(1), 50-61.

Traupmann, J., Petersen, R., Utne, M. & Hatfield, E. (1981). Measuring equity in intimate relations. *Applied Psychological Measurements,* 5(4), 467-480.

Truzzi, M. (Ed.). (1974). *Verstehen: Subjective understanding in social sciences.* Reading, Massachusetts: Addison-Wesley.

Tschann, J.M. (1988). Self-disclosure in adult friendships: Gender and marital status differences. *Journal of Social and Personal Relationships,* 5(1), 65-81.

Turk, H. & Simpson, R.L. (Eds.) *Institutions and social exchange: The sociologies of Talcott Parsons and George C. Homans.* Indianapolis: Bobbs-Merrill.

Vailliant, G.E. (1977). *Adaptation to life.* Boston: Little, Brown, and Co.

VanNieuwenhuljze, C.A.D. (1968). Reciprocity as a social science concept. In E.deVries (Ed.), *Essays on reciprocity.* Netherlands: Mouton & Co.

VanPeursen, C.A. (1968) Notes on a philosophy of reciprocity. In E. deVries (Ed.), *Essays on reciprocity.* Netherlands: Mouton & Co.

Van Vlissinger, J.F. (1970). Friendship in history. *Humanitas*, 6(2), 225-238.

Walster, E., Walster, G. & Berscheid, E. (1978). *Equity: Theory and research*. Boston: Allyn & Bacon.

Weber, M. (1958). *The Protestant ethic and spirit of capitalism*, T. Parsons (Trans.). New York: Charles Scribner's Sons.

Weinstein, E.A., DeVaughan, W.L., & Wiley, M.G. (1969). Obligation and the flow of deference in exchange. *Sociometry*, 32(1), 1-12.

Weiss, P. (1941). The golden rule. *The Journal of Philosophy*, 38(16), 421-430.

Weltner, L. (1978, January 29). Out of the closets and into friendship - the highest good. *Boston Globe*. New England section, p. 2.

Whyte, W.H. (1956). *The organization man*. New York: Doubleday.

Williams, P.C. (1973). *The principle of reciprocity*. Unpublished doctoral dissertation, Harvard University.

Wilmot, W.W. (1975). *Dyadic communications: A transactional perspective*. Reading, Massachusetts: Addison-Wesley.

Wiesman, J.P. (1986). Friendship: Bonds and binds in a voluntary relationship. *Journal of Social and Personal Relationships*, 3, 191-211.

Wolf, E.R. (1966). Kinship, friendship, and patron-client relationships in complex societies. In M. Banton (Ed.), *The social anthropology of complex societies* (pp. 1-20). New York: Frederick Praeger.

Wolff, G. (1977, May). Do you know who your friends are? and An illuminated history of a model friendship. *Esquire*.

Wong, H. (1981). Typologies of intimacy. *Psychology of Women Quarterly*, 5, 435-443.

Wright, P.H. (1974). The delineation and measurement of some key variables in the study of friendship. *Representative Research in Social Psychology*, 5, 93-96.

Wright, P.H. (1978). Toward a theory of friendship based on a conception of self. *Human Communication Research*, 4(3), 196-207.

Wright, P.H. (1982). Men's friendships, women's friendships and the alleged inferiority of the latter. *Sex Roles*, 8(1), 1-20.

Wright, P.H. (1988). Interpreting research on gender differences in friendship: A case for moderation and a plea for caution. *Journal of Social and Personal Relationships*, 5(3), 367-373.

Wright, P.H. & Crawford, A.C. (1971). Agreement and friendship: A close look and some second thoughts. *Representative Research in Social Psychology*, 2, 52-70.

Young, M. & Willmott, P. (1973). *The symmetrical family*. New York: Pantheon Books.

D1712089